The
Weatherford Collection

Donated by the family
of
Heiskell Weatherford

LORD OF THE FLIES

Fathers and Sons

TWAYNE'S MASTERWORK STUDIES

Robert Lecker, General Editor

LORD OF THE FLIES

Fathers and Sons

Patrick Reilly

TWAYNE PUBLISHERS • NEW YORK
Maxwell Macmillan Canada • Toronto
Maxwell Macmillan International • New York   Oxford
Singapore   Sydney

Twayne's Masterwork Studies No. 106

Lord of the Flies: Fathers and Sons
Patrick Reilly

Twayne Publishers   Maxwell Macmillan Canada, Inc.
Macmillan Publishing Company   1200 Eglinton Avenue East
866 Third Avenue   Suite 200
New York, New York 10022   Don Mills, Ontario M3C 3N1

Library of Congress Cataloging-in-Publication Data

Reilly, Patrick.
    Lord of the flies : fathers and sons / by Patrick Reilly.
        p.   cm. — (Twayne's masterwork studies ; no. 106)
    Includes bibliographical references and index.
    ISBN 0-8057-7999-X (HC : alk. paper)—ISBN 0-8057-8049-1 (PB : alk. paper)
    1. Golding, William, 1911–   Lord of the flies.   2. Fathers and sons in
literature.   I. Title.   II. Series.
PR6013.O35L664   1993
813'.914—dc20   92-30217
                                                                        CIP

The paper used in this publication meets the minimum requirements of American National Standard for Information Sciences—Permanence of Paper for Printed Library Materials. ANSI Z3948-1984. ∞ ™

10 9 8 7 6 5 4 3 2 1 (hc)
10 9 8 7 6 5 4 3 2 1 (pb)

Printed in the United States of America

CONTENTS

NOTE ON THE REFERENCES AND ACKNOWLEDGMENTS

Page references (in parentheses) are to the edition of *Lord of the Flies* published by Faber and Faber, London, in 1954. I am grateful to Faber for permission to quote from the text.

My overriding obligation is to my wife, Rose, for her patience and skill in preparing the manuscript. I should also like to thank Professors Michael DePorte, Christopher Fox, Carol Fabricant, Arthur Slaven, John Christie, Ronald Baker, Theodore Nostwich, and David Bruner for advice and support generously given during my teaching exchange year in the United States.

William Golding

Photograph by Caroline Forbes

CHRONOLOGY:
WILLIAM GOLDING'S LIFE AND WORKS

1911   William Golding born 19 September in St. Columb Minor,
              Cornwall, one of two sons of Alec Golding (soon to become
              senior assistant master at Marlborough Grammar School,
              Wiltshire) and Mildred Golding, an activist in the campaign
              for woman suffrage. The background is lower middle-class,
              the family one of schoolmasters. Once a pupil at his father's
              school, Golding has frequently acknowledged the overwhelm-
              ing influence of his father on his life. (See his essay, "The
              Ladder and the Tree," where he refers to his father as "incar-
              nate omniscience.") Alec wrote textbooks on various scientific
              subjects, including astrophysical navigation, played five musi-
              cal instruments, and was, in addition, a skilled carpenter and
              wood-carver. He campaigned for the Labour party but was
              never himself a candidate for office. He was a dedicated ratio-
              nalist, but not, according to his son, a scoffer at religion—
              rather, one who "regretted God so profoundly that he almost
              believed in Him." (Golding was to describe himself in 1970 as
              a non-Marxist Socialist, "*bitterly* left of centre.")[1]

1911–1918   Develops an interest in Egypt and archaeology that will be
              lifelong; at seven, learns hieroglyphics in order to write a play
              on Egypt (never completed). Coaxes mother while on visits to
              London to take him to the British Museum. While living in
              Wiltshire, visits Stonehenge and various churches and cathe-
              drals; finds in these early Christian, Saxon, and Norman re-
              mains an archaeological legacy to compare with Egypt.

1930   Enters Brasenose College, Oxford, well trained in science and
              able to play the piano, cello, oboe, violin, and viola. Reads
              science for two years before switching to English literature,
              having delayed so long because he thinks it will displease his
              father. This is a crucial career switch for Golding: see his essay
              "On the Crest of the Wave," in which he places the arts above
              science as a more important study for human beings. Golding
              is especially interested in Anglo-Saxon, in particular *The Battle*

of Maldon, a tenth-century heroic poem of stoic resistance to the Danes, ending in defeat. The switch from science to literature means that he takes an additional three years to complete his degree, in 1935; he also studies for a diploma in education.

1934   A friend sends 29 poems written by Golding to Macmillan; they are subsequently published as *Poems*. Some of these poems satirize the confidence of rationalism; others deal with the impossibility of reconciling the worlds of love and reason, the heart and the head. In the poem "Mr. Pope," Alexander Pope, as apostle of rationalism, complains to God that the world is not as ordered and precise as Pope would like it to be—the stars roam wild and free instead of dancing a minuet. (In his 1981 essay "My First Book," first published in *A Moving Target* (1982), Golding ironically remarks that his 34-page volume, remaindered in 1934, is now worth $4,000 in the United States.

1935   Graduates from Oxford. Writes, acts, and produces for a small, noncommercial theater in London, far from the West End. Plays the part of Danny, the sinister "hero" of Emlyn Williams's melodrama *Night Must Fall*. His experience here will later influence work such as *Pincher Martin* and *The Brass Butterfly*.

1939   Marries Ann Brookfield. Becomes schoolmaster at Bishop Wordsworth's School, Salisbury, teaching English and Greek literature in translation. Lives in a cottage in Wiltshire. Spends a great deal of time in adult education, traveling over the country, teaching in army camps and Maidstone Gaol.

1940–1945   Joins Royal Navy as an ordinary seaman after outbreak of World War II. Takes officer's examination and is so well versed in science (especially the study of propellants and explosives) that he is sent to work at a secret research center under Professor Lindemann (later Lord Cherwell), scientific adviser to Winston Churchill. Accidentally blows himself up and, after recovery, requests admiralty to send him back to sea, "where there's peace." (Golding's own words are that he "blew myself up" in an accident with detonators [See Biles, 27]. He was injured in an explosion and hospitalized.) Sent to a minesweeper school in Scotland and from there to New York to wait for a minesweeper being built on Long Island. Returns to Britain to find that the progress of the war means that minesweepers are no longer required. Given command of a small rocket-launching craft; involved in the chase and sinking

Chronology

of the *Bismarck*, and takes part in the D-Day assault upon Fortress Europe in 1944.

The war is crucial in Golding's moral and intellectual development. While at sea he begins to learn Greek, and Greek myth is to play a vital role in shaping his literary imagination—especially Euripides' *The Bacchae* on *Lord of the Flies* and Aeschylus's *Prometheus* on *Pincher Martin*. The war is his great educative experience: "one had one's nose rubbed in the human condition" (Biles, 33); it demolishes the remnants of naive, optimistic idealism, and demonstrates the wickedness of human nature. Golding attacks—in subsequent writing and interviews after the war—the complacency of the Allies in believing that only the Nazis committed war crimes (Biles, 34, 35–6).

1945–1961 Returns to Bishop Wordsworth's School to teach English and philosophy; he remains there until the success of *Lord of the Flies* enables him to retire and become a full-time writer. Begins to write derivative novels, none of which is accepted for publication. (In his essay "It's a Long Way to Oxyrhynchus," he laughs at his own determination to be published while being unable to find a publisher: he calls writing an addiction "with no Authors' Anonymous to wean you from the typewriter.") Has already written three unpublished novels by 1954, before his discovery that "you have to write your own novels."

1954 Faber and Faber publishes *Lord of the Flies* after more than 20 publishers had turned it down. Not an instantaneous public success but sufficiently encouraging to make him continue writing.

1955 Publishes *The Inheritors* (written in 28 days while teaching)—another strikingly original novel that stands H. G. Wells on his head. Elected a Fellow of the Royal Society of Literature.

1956 Publishes *Pincher Martin* (written in three weeks over a Christmas holiday). The novel is published in America as *The Two Deaths of Christopher Martin*, a title too revelatory of the plot. Some critics begin to make charges of gimmickry. Publishes a novella, *Envoy Extraordinary*, in a volume of three stories, together with John Wyndham and Mervyn Peake.

1958 His play *The Brass Butterfly* (adapted from *Envoy Extraordinary*) is performed in Oxford and London, with Alastair Sim in the chief role of the emperor. Dramatizes the clash between science and humanism, attacking the smug assumption of science that it can reshape human nature.

1959   *Free Fall* is published. Closer to a traditional novel than any of his previous books, it is not well received by the critics.

1960–1962   Frequent book reviewer and essayist for the *Spectator*. Begins to spend considerable time on his boat, cruising the English Channel, the Dutch coast, the North and Baltic seas.

1961   Resigns from his position as schoolmaster; has been busy with interviews and lectures, mainly on *Lord of the Flies*, now fast becoming a best-seller.

1961–1962   Spends a year as resident writer at Hollins College, Virginia, a rich girls' school in the Alleghenies.

1963   *Lord of the Flies* is made into a film, directed by Peter Brook.

1964   *The Spire* is published.

1965   A collection of essays, *The Hot Gates and Other Occasional Pieces*, is published, emphasizing, among other things, the importance of classical Greece to Golding's thought and art.

1966   Golding is made a C.B.E. (Commander of the British Empire).

1967   *The Pyramid* is published—an unusual book for Golding, with its evocation of the spirit of Anthony Trollope and the tradition of comic social fiction. Plans to sail to Greece in his own boat; the boat capsizes and is lost after a collision in the English Channel off the Isle of Wight. All on board are rescued by the Japanese ship that struck the boat.

1971   *The Scorpion God* is published—three novellas, including the already-published *Envoy Extraordinary*. The title story shows his preoccupation with the Egypt of mystery and darkness, the opposite of Greek rationalism and light. This polarity is recurrent throughout Golding's work.

1976   First visit to Egypt, accompanied by his wife in a car tour. A disappointing experience compounded by travel difficulties and illness.

1979   After a long silence, he publishes *Darkness Visible*. Signals the beginning of a new period of creativity and a revival of critical interest in his work.

1980   *Rites of Passage* is published and wins the Booker Prize for fiction.

1982   *A Moving Target* is published, a collection of essays that becomes the immediate occasion for his subsequent award of the Nobel Prize. Sees himself in the title essay as continually changing in his artistic response to experience—"Nothing Twice" is the motto.

Chronology

1983   Receives the Nobel Prize for fiction. The choice is attacked by a number of critics—as it had been in the case of John Steinbeck, whom Golding admired for the quality of his prose.

1984   *The Paper Men* is published. Second visit to Egypt; more interested in its buried past than in its slothful, dirty present.

1985   Publishes *An Egyptian Journal*, an account of his trip on a small boat down the Nile.

1987   *Close Quarters* is published—a "continuation" of *Rites of Passage*.

1989   *Fire Down Below* is published—a sequel to *Close Quarters*.

1990   New film version of *Lord of the Flies*, with American schoolboys replacing the English originals.

Literary and Historical Context

1

The Missing Master

In 1954, having already been rejected by 21 publishers, *Lord of the Flies* was published in England by Faber and Faber; one year later it appeared in the United States. Despite some respectful reviews, it had only a modest initial success. But within a surprisingly short time, it became a literary bombshell—acclaimed by the critics, its paperback selling in the millions throughout the English-speaking world. Frank Kermode hailed it as "a work of genius by a writer . . . in superbly full possession of his great powers";[1] on the other side of the Atlantic, Lionel Trilling pronounced it to be "one of the most striking literary phenomena of recent years," a book that had "captivated the imagination of a whole generation."[2] Golding's fellow practitioners were equally enthusiastic: "this remarkable book" was E. M. Forster's verdict (Page, 23), while Angus Wilson praised it for breathing new life into a fast atrophying form.[3]

Despite the books he has subsequently written, Golding is still best known as the author of *Lord of the Flies*. Anthony Burgess remarks that many people who claim to admire Golding have read only his first novel.[4] With unprecedented speed it established itself as a modern classic and acquired the ambiguous dignity of a prescribed text. It became a campus cult book, challenging and finally surpassing Salinger's *The Catcher in the Rye* as number one on the American literary charts. In 1963 it was made into a popular film and it has very recently been filmed again—among postwar novels, only Orwell's

Nineteen Eighty-four has been similarly honored. Its prodigious success enabled Golding to retire from schoolteaching and become a full-time writer, though he has commented wryly on how life cleverly got its own back by showering him with invitations from all over the world to lecture on his enduringly popular work: "My first novel ensured that I should be treated for the rest of my life as a schoolmaster."[5]

Golding tells us how the book came to be written—the particular occasion, the moment of conception, and the general matrix: the long years of brooding upon contemporary history that had gone to its creation. He and his wife were relaxing, having just put the children to bed after reading a boys' adventure story to them, when he happened to say, " 'Wouldn't it be a good idea if I wrote a story about boys on an island and let them behave as they really would?' She replied at once, 'That's a first class idea. You write it.' So I sat down and wrote it."[6] What, it is implied, could be simpler? But Golding tells us elsewhere that he wrote the novel as if tracing over words already on the page, and there can be no doubt that the work had been long germinating in his imagination, growing in the artistic womb.[7]

For the writing of *The Brothers Karamazov* Dostoyevski wrote to a friend who knew and loved children, asking him to supply the writer with all the advice and information the friend possessed on the subject; in addition, Dostoyevski studied the writings of Pestalozzi and Froebel.[8] Golding, father and schoolmaster, had no need to rely upon experts or secondary sources. He knew children as a professional; in an interview he speaks of occasions in school when only the master stands between his charges and mayhem: "He is God who stops a murder being committed."[9] The problem of authority bulks large in *Lord of the Flies*: what happens when the master is missing, when God is dead?

The problem was the more desperate because Golding had recently served in World War II, when the schoolroom of the world—masterless, bereft of authority—had been given over to the most monstrous mayhem. Murder had been committed on a massive scale by men, wicked children of a greater growth, who had elatedly discovered Dostoyevski's appalling truth: if there is no God, everything is permitted.[10] And in delicious abandon, they had acted upon it, much as Roger does in Golding's text. The war was the schoolroom in which Golding acquired his true education: "one had one's nose rubbed in the human condition" (Biles, 33). The experience was the more painful because Golding, as the son of good, rational, humanist parents—"how could

I talk to them about darkness and the irrational?"—(*Hot Gates*, 170) had been totally unprepared for it. He refers to his loss of belief in human perfectibility and in social engineering as the panacea for man's ills (*Moving*, 163).[11] How foolish to dream about the reorganization of society if man himself—not exceptional man, but average man—is sick (*Hot Gates*, 87): refurbishing a cancer ward will do nothing to cure the condition of its inmates. The war taught Golding that man is a morally diseased creature and the book it inspired was an attempt to trace the connection between man's diseased nature and the international mess he gets himself into (*Hot Gates*, 87): bad people make wars, not vice versa; the island does not destroy the boys, the boys destroy the island.

Explaining why Ralph must be kept alive at the end, Golding describes the theme of his book as the change from innocence—which is the ignorance of self—to a tragic knowledge.[12] *Lord of the Flies* is a schoolmaster's book, a work of instruction; not our children, but our children's parents are to be the targets of its pedagogy: "One of our faults is to believe that evil is somewhere else and inherent in another nation. My book was to say: you think that now the war is over and an evil thing destroyed, you are safe because you are naturally kind and decent" (*Hot Gates*, 89). In the text, the Lord of the Flies invites Simon to join him in mocking the folly of those who imagine that the beast is a thing that can be hunted down and destroyed—as crass a blunder as that of Brutus in believing that he can kill Caesarism by killing Caesar.

Golding's target is the myth of human innocence and the bad education that promotes it. The myth is particularly offensive in the smug self-congratulation of its English form: Golding will not permit his countrymen to dream themselves an immaculate conception in a world of evildoers. Only the accident of "certain social sanctions" or "social prohibitions" had, in Golding's view, prevented most people in Allied countries from behaving like Nazis (Biles, 36). For Golding there is no *essential* difference between the Allies and the Nazis, the "good" and the "bad": *we* could so easily be *them*. The most dramatic demonstration of this truth in the novel is the slaughter of Simon: Golding ensures that the "good" boys, Ralph and Piggy, play as hideously full a part in the atrocity as the "bad" boys, Jack and Roger. It is one of the worst consequences of our bad education that we can believe such asininities as the segregation of the world into wicked people (our enemies) and virtuous people (ourselves). Golding's vocation as schoolmaster makes him vitally interested in the subject of education; the chauvinist nonsense spoken by Jack is simply the egregious extreme of a shared delusion, a folly held in common with the other boys.[13]

Lord of the Flies must be located within its historical context as the prelude to a proper understanding. Golding tells us that it was "written at a time of great world grief."[14] The fallacious idea of an easily written book, perhaps encouraged by Golding in his remark about tracing over words already on the page, is dispelled by Golding's reference to "years of wordless brooding that brought me not so much to an opinion as a stance. It was like lamenting the lost childhood of the world. . . . The theme of Lord of the Flies is grief, sheer grief, grief, grief, grief, grief" (Moving, 163).

The surprising resonance evoked by Golding's deceptively simple narrative testifies to the work's incontestable timeliness, and it is true that the book finely dramatized anxieties common to a postwar world.[15] But that world now belongs to history and the book still speaks to our condition. It is, clearly, not just a tract for the times, restricted to its historical moment, but a fable of timeless import, transcending its immediate occasion. It is inadequate to say that, because of its reactionary or illiberal view of man, Lord of the Flies struck deep into a variety of twentieth-century ganglia—as though critical and audience acclaim could be so easily secured.[16] It is puerile to describe the book as a product of wartime disillusion or to dismiss it as a retreat into allegory from the problems of the modern world— if that were so, its vogue would have been short-lived.[17] The book exhibits the darkness of man's heart, not the temporary malaise of one historical disaster. To argue that Lord of the Flies is only relevant to or is limited by World War II is about as sensible as attempting to confine Candide to a meditation on the Lisbon earthquake.

The work transcends its occasion, is a matter of permanent truth rather than of transient excitement, and this is true not only of its all too visible darkness, but also of its generally unrecognized light. Despite being written at a time of great world grief, Lord of the Flies is, nevertheless, not a work of unrelieved despair. Golding remarks that the glum intellect has nothing to say of the fairy prince and the sleeping beauty, but much to say of the tower and the dungeon (Moving, 186). He complains, with some justification, that while everyone noticed the original sin in the novel, nobody noticed the original virtue (Rosso). In this study I attempt to present Lord of the Flies as a work, not of the glum intellect, but of the joyful imagination. One of my prime purposes will be to show the virtue as well as the sin, to do justice to the prince as well as to the dungeon.

2

The Failed Schoolroom

Lord of the Flies is one of the most important texts of the twentieth century, for both literary and extraliterary reasons. It is a fable vital to our times for three reasons: the urgency of its questions, the audacity of its answers, and the formal originality of its investigation.

The urgency is self-evident. Here, thinly disguised as a boys' adventure story, is a searching analysis of the human situation, a profound parable of man's condition. "What are we? Humans? Or animals? Or savages?" Piggy rages as the assembly lurches toward darkness, and his questions are not restricted to the wicked child's-play of beastly boys on a tropic island (99). "What's wrong?"—Ralph's anguished plea for enlightenment reverberates through the dark annals of twentieth-century history, the century of gas-ovens, gulags and genocide (154). "What makes things break up like they do?"—is there a more important query or one upon whose correct solution so much depends (154)? Golding's tale rules out any behaviorist or economic answer: the struggle to survive is moral, not physical. It is about staying human even more than staying alive; it is about the meaning, not the means, of life. *Lord of the Flies* is a tragedy of human nature, not of environment.

"Things are breaking up. I don't understand why. We began well; we were happy. And then—" Ralph's sheer bafflement compels us to ponder the efficacy of the education that leaves him so helpless; and it is *our* education as well as his that is on the line (89). Piggy's facile answer—that Jack is the sole culprit, that a handful of charismatically evil enchanters (Stalin, Hitler, and the like) have somehow ruined the world—will not serve (154). Piggy stands for an especially egregious failure in that miseducation that has merely intensified our predicament. Freedom, education, science—these are the three great pieties of the modern West: in *Lord of the Flies* each is subjected to a searching critique.

In analyzing the reason for Piggy's failure, we confront the first great scandal of the book, the shockingly subversive attitude toward science and technology exhibited therein. Piggy, remarks Golding ungenerously, is the kind of person who will end up in a white coat at Los Alamos (Biles, 14). In the text Piggy is a decent, well-meaning, victimized boy, but Golding's injustice serves to highlight what is most culpable in Piggy's outlook: a naive and potentially disastrous faith in science. Golding's own decision, taken at university, to defect from science to English literature, is a key to unlock his writings. What must have struck him as a sort of apostasy, almost a treachery (however unavoidable and finally justifiable)—he delayed the switch because "it would hurt my father so much" (Biles, 89–90)—is comparable to Orwell's quasi-parricidal rejection of H. G. Wells.[1] Golding knew what it would cost. "To attack 'Science' is to be labelled reactionary; and to applaud it, the way to an easy popularity" (*Hot Gates*, 129). In the age of Harold Wilson's technological revolution, when science and education had become virtually synonymous terms, it was a risky thing to do, and some of the most savage criticism of Golding has come from the outraged champions of science.[2] Nevertheless, Golding heretically insists that science is *not* the paramount human activity, defiantly ranking philosophy, history, and aesthetic perception as both higher and more essential pursuits (*Hot Gates*, 130). If man is a species that produces evil as a bee produces honey, his unfettered control over the powers of nature may be cause for dread rather than delectation (*Hot Gates*, 87). When Jack becomes Prometheus, the thief of fire, he uses his newly acquired technology to torch the island: what the child can do, the man can surpass. It is scarcely confirmation of the belief that science is the savior.

Science is but one branch of an education that has gone woefully astray. The contrast between *Lord of the Flies* and *The Catcher in the Rye* as radically opposed versions of man's estate is pertinent here. *Catcher* is a Rousseau-inspired text of an innocent victimized by a corrupt society, a sentimentally consoling reiteration of the moral man/ immoral society antithesis; *Lord of the Flies* is about the darkness within: "Fancy thinking the Beast was something you could hunt and kill!" (158). Despite the Lord's derisive incredulity, the conviction that evil is primarily a social phenomenon is, nevertheless, *the* salient moral imbecility of our civilization and its sustaining education; but it is also, significantly, a folly from which Simon is laudably exempt—somehow, miraculously, he has escaped the bad education of the other boys.

Simon's centrality to the text is related to its second great scandal, the sheer inadequacy of what passes among us for education. If we are to believe Golding, it is precisely the literate and intelligent in our society who are most ruinously misled, since it is they who cannot understand Simon; the illiterate person, who knows about saints and sanctity, has no such difficulty. Golding rejects the description of Simon as scapegoat as smacking too much of Golden Bough reductionism; Simon is a saint, a proof that God exists: no God, no Simon—the illiterate person, who has not been educated to hope for the worst, easily understands this (Kermode, "Meanings" 9; *Puzzles*, 201). Our modern idea of a saint (even when we consent to the term) is inseparable from ideals of public service: Mother Theresa is a saint because she helps people, not because she serves God. Simon serves the community, no one better ("Simon helps" [59]), but he transcends society, is not to be comprehended within it. His knowledge of and intimacy with nature is of an intuitive, irrational kind, impossible to reconcile with the accredited and highly successful methods of the physical sciences. Golding presents us with only two alternatives for Simon: to dismiss him as a holy imbecile, incomprehensible and irrelevant; or to concede that there are modes of knowing different from and perhaps superior to those based on rational insight and mathematical reasoning. It should not surprise us that so many readers are impatient with Simon; they feel toward this subverter of established pieties as any zealot of the Age of Faith felt toward the disturber of *his* religion.

True education (of which Simon is Golding's exemplar) is crucial to the book: Golding declined the description of *Lord of the Flies* as a kind of black mass version of Ballantyne—it is, he insisted, a *realistic* view of the Ballantyne situation (Kermode, "Meaning," 10). Hence the attack upon the third great shibboleth of modern culture, the inadequate and superficial view of human freedom that it propounds. We no longer see man against a background of values or realities that transcend him[3]: nothing transcends him, he is autonomous man, the measure of all things, the sole intelligence, so far as we know, in an otherwise mindless universe. Our modern liberal moral theory exalts human freedom in discarding the archaic background of values, encouraging us to believe that we are totally free, knowing everything we need to know for the important purposes of life. Our naive trust in technology breeds a contempt for reality, a casually arrogant assumption that the real world is easily known and just as easily mastered. Truth is the great casualty of this attitude, sacrificed in the scientific world to utility, in the moral world to sincerity.

No mistake could be more perilous. Education is more than information retrieval (man, insisted Dr. Johnson, needs reminding more than information) or acquiring the techniques to manipulate matter—know thyself, said the Greeks, to whom Golding is so indebted. To become truly free is a much more complex and difficult matter than J. S. Mill allows. Golding's boys will learn in pain and terror that they are not the splendid free choosers, the monarchs of all they survey, which a false education has duped them to believe. This false idea of freedom fosters a dreamlike facility, whereas what we require is a renewed sense of the difficulty and complexity of the moral life and the opacity, perhaps even the evil, of people. It is because the boys take exile too lightly, dream of rescue too easily, that they fail so catastrophically.

In Golding, the art of invention is inseparable from the impulse toward instruction; the extraliterary importance of literature, for him, is that it can take over some of the tasks formerly performed by philosophy and religion. It can help us to rediscover the lost density of our lives, can arm us against fantasy (R. M. Ballantyne's *The Coral Island* is an especially indefensible example, but there are others, less flagrant and therefore far more dangerous), and can defend us against the errors of an entrenched but mistaken education. Freedom, says Rousseau, is delicious to eat but hard to digest: *Lord of the Flies* shows how serious the gastric disorder can be. Golding is, it must be conceded, not primarily interested in the body and pressure of lived life in a wide society, and those who desiderate this must go elsewhere. But he rightly objected when it was put to him that his books are concerned with either persons or societies *unnaturally* isolated: *conveniently*, is his preferred term (Kermode, "Meaning," 9).

The prime purpose of this study is to justify Golding's use of this word. When a sick person visits a doctor, it is convenient for the examination that the patient should strip. This is not because the doctor despises clothes or thinks them unimportant or disposable; they may be very elegant clothes which the patient may treasure and the doctor admire—but they get in the way of the examination. We must disrobe if we are to learn the truth of our condition. *Lord of the Flies* is such a disrobing. To simplify without oversimplifying: it is perhaps the most taxing, most difficult art of all. There is very little point, says Golding, in writing a novel unless you do either something that you suspected you could not do, or something that you are pretty certain nobody else has tried before; if you see as everybody else sees, there is no point in writing the book (Kermode, "Meaning," 10). *Lord of the Flies* triumphantly fulfills the prescription: it is not only novel, but audaciously and shiningly so.

3

The Strife of the Critics

"I am a man more analysed than analysing" (*Moving*, 171): the woe-begone words and martyred tone reveal Golding savoring the joke as he incongruously dons the mantle of the injured Lear, but to anyone confronting the mass of critical commentary now fastened to *Lord of the Flies* the joke lies on a bedrock of truth. What must be added is that some of the analysis is self-analysis, since Golding has contributed in no small degree to the debate—he writes, self-mockingly, of having gone near to surrounding *Lord of the Flies* with commentary much as Dante did with the *Vita Nuova* (*Moving*, 172). Nevertheless, despite his own input, he ruefully records the fact that he has become "the raw material of an academic light industry," that "the books that have been written about my books have made a statue of me," that it is "a melancholy thought that I have become a school textbook before I am properly dead and buried" (*Moving*, 169; *Hot Gates*, 101). (His enemies, as we shall see, regard it as deplorable that his work should ever be given to the young at all.) His dislike of being "posted into a pigeonhole like a letter" (*Moving*, 183), reinforced by a sense of how ludicrously inappropriate much of this explication is, doubtless lies behind his breezy denial of ever having read Freud and his protest at his text being summoned to appear before Aquinas: "It has been painfully and wryly amusing to me when people throw things like the *Summa* at my poor little boys. . . . Isn't it cracking an opusculum with a critical sledgehammer?"[1] It is hard to tell whether irritation or modesty is in the ascendant.

Yet one must conclude that something about his poor little boys has from the outset irresistibly attracted the kind of speculation over which Golding shakes his head, and the "fault," if it be so, is surely not always that of the speculator: according to David Skilton, "The chief danger with Golding's novels is that they invite interpretation" (Page, 151). Perhaps—but then what should they invite? *Lord of the Flies* is undeniably a text that, however superficially simple, invites, indeed compels, its reader to seek some deeper explanation, some secret significance, concealed beneath the overt events of its story. The overall intention may, as Golding insists, be stated simply enough, but he, too, has been forced to concede, in the face of its critical reception, that it is a book at once highly and diversely explicable: hospitable to Freudian, neo-Freudian, and Jungian analysis, to Roman Catholic approval (Golding must surely have also heard the murmurs of Roman Catholic disapproval), to Protestant appraisal and to nonconformist surmise, to scientific humanist misinterpretation, and to the frog-marching and manipulations of the two dialectics—Hegelian and Marxist (*Moving*, 171). If Golding intended the list as a reductio ad absurdum, it curiously misfires; instead of exposing the folly of the exegetes, it highlights the openness of the text as somehow fulfilling the Gospel exhortation to be all things to all men. So, at any rate, it has proved. *Lord of the Flies* has been read as a moral fable of personal disintegration, as a social fable of communal regression, as a religious fable of the fall of man. Golding's own explicit surrender of any *patria potestas* over his books, his sensible decision to let them leave home and take their chances in the world as all healthy children finally must, his admission that the critic may legitimately find in a text something that the author may never have noticed or intended (*Hot Gates*, 100)— all of this leaves *Lord of the Flies* temptingly exposed in the arena as a prize for which the critical gladiators will inevitably contend.

Those who condemn the book as overly explicit, thin, too obviously contrived, must tell us what kind of fable it is whose moral cannot, apparently, be read aright. We confront the paradox of an allegedly simple book—everyone agrees on this, admirers and detractors alike, those who extol the simplicity and those who rebuke it— that is somehow capable of provoking the deepest, most irreconcilable disagreements. What use to remark that "despite the roar of baffled critics, Mr. Golding's intentions are always simple" (Kermode, *Puzzles*, 198)? If the critics are baffled, how can the intentions be simple?

If the intentions are simple, why are the critics baffled? The truth is that the critics are not baffled, but at loggerheads. Everyone apparently knows the meaning of *Lord of the Flies*, including the critic who incredibly upbraids Golding for being too deferential to the authority of science[2]—it is simply that one man's meaning is another's aberration. In tiny detail as in overall theme the same stark collision of view is apparent. One critic takes the decision to move the signal fire from the beast-possessed mountain to the beach as proof of Piggy's intellectual prowess and audacity; others see here Golding's mocking confirmation of Piggy's inferiority to Simon. Golding's simplicity of intention is evidently of a kind guaranteed to foment dissension and dispute. Graham Hough, deploring *Free Fall* as a sad departure from the kind of novel at which Golding excels, contrastingly praises *Lord of the Flies* for its "force and vividness in the application of truths that we all know" (Page, 27). Anyone surveying the startling antagonisms, the head-on, radical divergences in the spectrum of interpretation provoked by this book, might be forgiven for believing that this was written tongue in cheek.

The book has been read as exhibiting both guarded optimism and total pessimism: one critic "knows" that it depicts the triumph of civilization over the beast, another declares that only an idiot will suppose that it ends happily.[3] It is praised as an implicit tribute to the humanizing power of social institutions, an antiprimitivist tract, and berated as the work of a primitive romantic, sullenly hostile to science and progress, an especially cankered example of C. P. Snow's literary malcontent (Martin Green, 453–54). Golding has been identified as an existentialist who places man in contingent situations in order to test scientific and religious orthodoxies, subjecting dogma to experience, and also as an incisive contributor to a debate in political theory, his characters being symbols of diverse responses to the question of authority.[4] Golding himself has said that his book, revoking Rousseau, traces the defects of society back to the defects of human nature (Nelson, 172); others object that it shows, rather, the evils within Western culture. Still others, from the New Left, protest that the beast denotes a pernicious system rather than any evil inherent in man.[5]

A major crux is whether Golding is religious or atheist, with those who opt for the first alternative divided as to the kind of religion he believes. Some deny the relevance of traditional Christianity altogether, finding the Greeks, and, in particular, the Apollonian-Dionysian polarity, to be the most fruitful source for *Lord of the Flies*: we read it with the help of *The Bacchae*.[6] One major school interprets the text in terms of traditional Christian symbolism, identifying Golding as that rarity in English literature, a religious novelist whose concerns are the eternal spiritual questions—*Lord of the Flies* is a moral work, compatible with, if not limited to, the orthodox doctrine of original sin (Hynes, 16). Others find the Christianity present but in curiously heterodox form: Golding's real achievement has been to produce his own myths from a compost of Christian teaching.[7] It has been argued that although the novels do not make sense except from the pen of a Christian writer, the crucial element of salvation is missing[8]; others point out that the "official" representatives of Christianity tend to show up badly in Golding's books—the head choirboy is Beelzebub's high priest.[9] But, predictably, as with a writer where every critical yea provokes its competing nay, Golding has been presented as a believer, not just in Beelzebub, the Fall, and paradise lost, but also in divine mercy (Kermode, *Puzzles* 202). One is left wondering how such a "simple" book has set its readers so violently at variance.

Every conceivable reading seems to have its supporters. We are offered a Manichaean Golding, pessimistic to the core, believing in Beelzebub, but not in Beelzebub's master.[10] The book has divided Christian from atheist, Christian from Christian, Catholic from Catholic. Catholic critics in the United States were split between those who mourned the best-selling triumph over *The Catcher in the Rye* as a sad evidence that humane liberalism had lost its campus battle with Calvinist despair, and those who embraced the book for its emphasis on individual responsibility and its laudable refusal to countenance the modern alibi of environmental servitude.[11] Far from blaming him for a demoralizing surrender to total depravity, such readers praised him for targeting, in commendably orthodox style, the harmful humanist heresies of self-sufficiency, natural innocence, and earthly perfectibility. Golding's influence upon the young, as demonstrated in his book's triumph as lord of the campus, was at the root of the debate. The denunciation of Golding as literary pied piper, leading the young disastrously astray with his despairing melodies, appears at its most extreme in R. C. Townsend, the most virulent of the naysayers.[12] According to Townsend, Golding does not only shamelessly exploit his children-characters, manipulating them to suit his pernicious thesis; more culpably still, he has exploited his young readers, those too-easily disillusioned innocents who fall into the trap of his facile, fashionable pessimism, his boutique despair. So fierce is Townsend's onslaught that one almost expects to hear him quote Christ's terrible words concerning the *Kinderschander*, the scandalizer of the young: better for such a man that he be bound and cast into the depths of the sea. The "truths that we all know" are, it seems, protean enough to set the critics at each other's throats.

The same fierce antagonisms are provoked by the form as by the content of *Lord of the Flies*. Repeatedly, terms such as fable, allegory, parable, and romance are used, and much of the animus concentrated in such description has to do with an assumption that such work is mechanical, prefabricated and predetermined: what seems to be alive, with a will of its own, is discovered on inspection to be android, with every motion directed by an outside agent. The authentic novelist discovers the truth of his work, the path it will take, the shape it will assume, in the creative process—he listens to it and it tells him where it wants to go. The artist is really a midwife, helping to deliver something that has a being and a purpose of its own; far from being the god of this creation, he is simply the accoucheur. The novel writes itself, and the two most illustrative instances of this autonomy come, appropriately, from our two master novelists, Tolstoy and Dostoyevski. Immersed in *Anna Karenina*, Tolstoy writes in deep amazement to a friend that Vronsky has shocked him by attempting suicide[13]—an act completely at odds with Tolstoy's expectations: when a character is truly free, he will do his own thing. In *Crime and Punishment* we watch as Dostoyevski discovers with Raskolnikov the true motive for the old pawnbroker's murder: the murderer proposes, only to dismiss, the specious utilitarian rationale and the equally specious "Napoleonic" justification before finally stumbling upon the truth, a truth as surprising to Dostoyevsky as to himself—he just wanted to do it. Truth comes only at the end, after the struggle—never as a free gift at the start.

The fabulist, by contrast, so it is alleged, reverses the imaginative order: he knows in advance the truth he seeks; the destination perversely precedes the journey. There is no sense of discovery: how could there be when the writer rigidly shapes his work according to the specifications of the blueprint in his head? He is an engineer, a technician, and, however beautifully or cunningly contrived, it is not a living thing that comes from his lathe, but a manufacture, an artifact. The sense of felt life, of newness, discovery, revelation, are missing from even the best of fables. From the beginning, some such complaint has echoed through the critical debate on *Lord of the Flies*. The novel has been attacked as oversimplified, overexplicit, theme-ridden, schematic, diagrammatic—a kind of literary experiment reeking of the scientific laboratory that Golding thought he had forsaken.[14] Golding himself lends credence to such a view by describing himself as a kind of literary scientist, an engineer of human nature, isolating his material in controlled conditions much as his white-coated counterparts do when testing the tensile strength of metals and concretes by subjecting them to artificially contrived pressures (*Moving*, 199). *Lord of the Flies* tests our culture by transplanting it to an exotic locale where it prospers or withers depending upon its intrinsic durability and strength. *Gulliver's Travels* is the great prototype of such fictions, and Joseph Conrad, Joyce Cary, and Graham Greene have in this century made striking contributions to the genre.

These distinguished names notwithstanding, some readers remain uneasy with the basic enterprise. If the threat to "true" fiction is that, in staying faithful to the complexity of life, it may become so confused as to lose all shape and organization, the hazard of fable is that it will be insufficiently clothed in the garment of actuality, that it will be too bare, too fettered by preexisting intentions, to come alive.[15] Such fictions are encoded messages, illustrations of conclusions already reached, the fleshing out of abstractions, ideas dressed up as people. They leave the impression that their purpose is anterior, some initial thesis or contention that they are apparently concerned to embody and express in concrete form. Their didacticism has a tendency to reduce life to pattern.

Golding has been arraigned on all of these charges: he has been called a "tricky" writer, theme-ridden and overacademic, a heavy-handed fabulist with a derivative or eccentric vision, a contriver of gimmicks.[16] The plot of *Lord of the Flies* has been attacked as both eccentric and specious—either too far removed from the real world or too neatly microscopic to be true (Johnston, 18). The occupational hazard of such fiction—that the thesis is incompletely translated into the story, with the result that much remains external and extrinsic, a teller's assertion rather than a tale's enactment—is the gravamen against Golding. Regrettably, Golding has occasionally helped to convict himself, as, for example, in his retrospective explication of the dead parachutist as history, "the thing which is dead but won't lie down," that legacy from the past that frustrates our future salvation (*Hot Gates*, 95). Not only is this "academic" in the bad sense, not only unconvincing and redundant—worse still, it contradicts our impression in reading the text. Simon's pity and reverence are directed, not to history, but to a poor dead man, harmless and horrible: this is what the *text* says, and Golding's later explication is both otiose and wayward.

But much more is at stake than Golding's very infrequent and unwelcome second thoughts, especially when so much of what he says is both helpful and illuminating. The argument his defenders must respond to is that he is the kind of allegorist who creates a fable to depict certain a priori perceptions about the human condition, and that, since he is reprehensibly more concerned with theme than credibility, the puppet-master's strings are all too plainly perceptible. The pied piper, who leads his reader-children astray, is a Procrustes toward his character-children, ruthlessly shaping them to fit his story: "his authorial presence is often overly obtrusive, either in didactic interpositions or, more seriously, in unconvincing manipulation of his characters" (Johnston, 10)—a particularly offensive example being the scenes involving Simon and the Beast. Another instance cited is when Piggy denies the existence of ghosts because things must make sense (101). Despite being cleverly camouflaged in boyish diction, the ventriloquism, so it is alleged, is glaring: a boy of ten could never reason like this (Johnston, 11). The freedom of Vronsky and Raskolnikov is depressingly absent: Golding's characters run like little clockwork-figures on the predictable grooves of their maker's contriving.

For those who believe this, Golding's own countertestimony will count for little. Nevertheless, Golding is on record as insisting that the art of *Lord of the Flies* is that of discovery and not communication. He has cited the Beast's warning to Simon as precisely the epiphanic moment, the Vronsky moment, in his tale: "I was writing at his dictation. . . . It was at this point of imaginative concentration that I found that the pig's head knew Simon was there" (*Hot Gates*, 98). Here is Golding listening intently to his own story to hear what it wants to be—precisely what his detractors say he never does. A fable can be so easily controlled to death; but what has been said of *The Spire* is equally applicable to *Lord of the Flies*: "meanings that grow out of the fiction and are not imposed from without."[17] Golding speculates that these moments of imaginative plenitude, of overflowing, when the fable comes to its own life, are the most valuable of all: "where I thought it was failing, it was really succeeding" (*Hot Gates*, 100).

A host of critical witnesses have testified to the truth of this. Some resolve the sterile dispute between fable and fiction by finding in *Lord of the Flies* a fertile union of the two—the text does not assert an abstract proposition, but creates a vivid fictional world that *shows* rather than *tells* Golding's truth.[18] The conch is adduced as one illustrative instance of this harmonious union of symbol and concrete detail, the ability to embody moral meaning in artistic form. Experience, not statement, is the clue to Golding: he is a maker of myths, not a debater of doctrines. His descriptive prose not only carries the burden of his meaning but presents this meaning in a process of discovery for author and reader alike: "the intensely disturbing force of his own fiction came to him as a surprise. He was the first horrified observer of the ruthless boys he gave birth to."[19] For such critics the realities of *Lord of the Flies* live in the flesh as well as in the abstract, simply because Golding never forgets the concrete in his search for symbolic action. Golding recounts the origin of his book in a remark made to his wife: "Wouldn't it be a good idea if I wrote a story about boys on an island and let them behave as they really would?"; and he also speaks of an ambition to create "real boys instead of paper cutouts with no life in them" (*Hot Gates*, 88). Against those who accuse him of making the boys dance to his allegorical tune, his admirers point to his remarkable awareness of the realities of the playground world: "The story is more striking precisely because Golding chooses wonderfully real children as protagonists, children who yank up socks, stamp feet, and quarrel over sand castles" (Tiger, 53). Against those who find the vampire—theme—sucking the blood from life, his admirers hail the intense physical immediacy of Golding's world: "Whatever they may symbolise his schoolboys . . . exist as sharply differentiated individuals" (Green, 57). It is no more Golding's fault than it is Bunyan's, if people insist on misreading their books, cutting through and destroying their abundant life in the foolish hope of reaching some alleged inner, cryptogrammatic meaning. Inner meaning is inseparable from outer life; we possess both or none at all.

Even those critics who deplore the modern preference for fable as a mark of decadence are driven, albeit grudgingly, to concede the saving originality of Golding's achievement. John Peter, lamenting that so gifted a writer as Golding should have forsaken the plenitude of fiction for the narrowness of fable, speculates that some future critic may well esteem a moderate success in fiction, such as Angus Wilson's *Anglo-Saxon Attitudes* (1956), above any of the fables contemporary with it, no matter how finely done. Yet Peter concludes his essay in generous acknowledgment that Golding has "done more for the modern British novel than any of the recent novelists who have emerged. More, it may be, than all of them" (Peter, 592).

The allusion to Angus Wilson is especially ironic in the light of his own misgivings concerning the contemporary English novel (Wilson, 238–51). For him it is too provincial, too subservient to middle-class views of right and wrong to be able to explain human conduct; the novel of manners, great pedigree notwithstanding, has become an increasingly restrictive influence, with its well-bred disregard of the problem of evil. The result has been to reduce the novel to an intelligent, humorous, well-observed sociology—a *felt* sociology, but no more. This superior journalism, the degenerate descendant of the great nineteenth-century novel, telling, with pale, conventional characters, some straightforward story enlivened with empirical facts, is at risk of falling into disrepute. Wilson argues that the traditional novel has become too easy (he offers to write half a dozen within a given period)—it is simply a matter of competence, the novelist's to write, the reader's to read. Social realism has become the refuge of the novelist without vocation: "we have to reject the idea of the traditional novel being all that we have" (Wilson, 245).

Into this artistic somnolence burst *Lord of the Flies* in 1954. Wilson praises Golding as the English writer who has been most successful in solving the problem of expressing transcendent good and evil, in dealing with the overspill that goes beyond mere social right and wrong (Wilson, 21). The advocates of the antinovel insist that a new writer's task is the correction of obsolete versions of reality imposed by earlier novels. Golding is, in a sense, an antinovelist, engaged in epistemological correction. Describing how he came to write *The Spire*, Golding tells of the cathedral spire that dominated the town in which he lived—but then adds that there was also a gasworks. "Why did I not choose the gasworks? I can think of a number of contemporaries who would have chosen the gasworks" (*Moving*, 166). Golding, clearly, is the kind of novelist who will always prefer spire to gasworks, for he finds nothing in the latter to nourish his imagination. He disdains "gasworks" fiction, the fiction of the contemporary world of sex and class, not because it is untrue—rather that it is pointless and irresponsible, as though a man with a brain tumor were to worry about his hairstyle. Wilson's exhortation to break out of the prison of traditional fiction is a pointer to Golding's achievement, since there has been no more startling escapee; whatever else is said, no one will deny that he has written his own books.

They are his; and they are *written*. In an age when eloquence is unfashionable, when even "style," except in the most austere sense of the word, is frowned upon, Golding has the courage to endow prose with an imaginative function usually reserved for poetry. Our tendency is to undervalue prose as an instrument of the imagination: prose is for exposition and explanation—it is essentially didactic, documentary, informative. The pity is that we have to use words at all—our secret nostalgia is that of Swift's linguistic reformers in the Academy of Lagado, who would dispense with words altogether in favor of things.[20] But, since words are a necessary evil, the barer and the more starkly transparent they are the better. Prose is a windowpane that we look *through*, not *at*—Hemingway is our great modern stylist. We feel embarrassed at eloquence as at an indecency, discomfited with a prose animated with the energies of poetry (Murdoch, 28–29).

Golding, however, has no dread of rhetoric, is drawn to rather than deterred by poetry. In addition to reviving a moribund novel with a new and exciting subject (Koestler describes *The Inheritors* as an earthquake in the petrified forests of the English novel), he has also reinvigorated the language with a new and more eloquent mode of discourse. He is a poetic novelist, relying massively upon theme, imagery, and symbolism, much as Shakespeare (whom he claims as a great forerunner) does.[21] In restoring to prose the qualities of poetry, Golding takes great risks, notably in the set pieces involving Simon as solitary: his communing with nature, his encounter with the Beast, the resumption of his corpse by the solicitous ocean. We make rhetoric out of our quarrel with others, says Yeats, poetry out of our quarrel with ourselves.[22] Golding is at his most poetic when Simon is alone. It is appropriate that Golding's detractors should find such passages the most objectionable, while his admirers, by contrast, advance them as the apex of his achievement. Nothing could more illuminatingly reveal the impassable gulf between the two sides.

A Reading

4

Gulliver's Legacy

"I am groping for an answer to the question, how such a writer can strike us as profoundly attuned to contemporary sensibility?" (Kermode, *Puzzles*, 200). Kermode's frank puzzlement is the more intriguing for having come from a critic whose admiration for Golding is unstinted—who was, indeed, one of the first to call attention to the power of his achievement. The clue lies within the phrase "such a writer." For Kermode, Golding is a maverick, deviser of outré and startlingly original themes, almost an antinovelist in the light of his disdainful disregard of the long-established conventions of the genre. This view, advanced from the outset by admirers and censurers alike, finds apparent validation in Golding's own words: "I think that my novels have very little genesis outside myself. That to a large extent I've cut myself off from contemporary literary life, and gained in one sense by it, though I may have lost in another" (Kermode, *Puzzles*, 199). Coming from a writer who has been described as a literary counterpuncher, a reactionary in the literal sense of needing an adversary, be it Ballantyne, Wells, or Defoe, to stimulate his own creative imagination, this may seem at first glance a surprising statement—although a major aim of this study will be to vindicate its truth (Oldsey and Weintraub, 34–35).

Nevertheless, there is something misleading in regarding Golding as a case of literary parthenogenesis—viewing him as an *isolato,* incommunicado in the modern world, immured within his own sensibility, his works springing unprompted from his brain like Pallas Athena from the head of Zeus. The aim of this chapter is twofold: to locate him within a climate of opinion where his work, with no slight to its originality, can be situated in relation to certain other significant twentieth-century texts; and to place him within a highly reputable tradition of fiction that finds its origin in *Gulliver's Travels* and that continues to bear fruit in such outstanding modern writers as Conrad, Orwell, and Camus. In considering why the intellectual climate of our times should be so warmly hospitable to Swift's masterpiece, making it so relevant as to be almost contemporary, the intention is simultaneously to demonstrate the potency of Golding's appeal to modern readers, that appeal which Kermode recognizes but is hard-pressed to explain.

I have argued elsewhere that a salient, almost a defining, characteristic of modern literature, stunningly reiterated in some of the major texts of our day—*Heart of Darkness, Death in Venice, The Trial, Darkness at Noon, Nineteen Eighty-four, The Fall*—is a Judas moment when the self is suddenly stricken by a sense of its own vileness, a negative or dark epiphany when the vision is one of loss rather than salvation, of abandonment rather than rescue.[1] To be made aware of one's own worthlessness, to gag at one's own corruption, has become in our fiction almost a paradigmatic experience, and here our literature stands radically opposed to that of the preceding century. There the concomitant experience is one of forgiveness and redemption, mercy rendered and received, sin expiated and overcome. Our own century, for obvious reasons, has increasingly come to disbelieve in this redemptive moment—the moment of the Ancient Mariner, Jean Valjean, Silas Marner, Gwendolen Harleth, Sydney Carton, Dombey, Raskolnikov, Dmitry Karamazov, Pierre Bezuhov—so confidently announced in the ultimately optimistic art of the nineteenth century. Our age—it should not surprise us—is far less responsive than its predecessor to the promise of salvation, far less committed to the avoidance of tragedy that was the prime requirement of Victorian sensibility.

The very titles are revelatory. George Eliot writes *Janet's Repentance*—it needs only a change of possessive to make it applicable to so many key works of the time; Tolstoy calls his last great novel *Resurrection*, thereby giving explicit religious form to the underlying hope of his century. In this literature, however harsh the narrative, the end is almost always a reconciliation—that *Madame Bovary, L'Assommoir*, and *Tess of the d'Urbervilles* are here so scandalously heretical marks them as the subversive harbingers of a bleaker future, abhorred and vilified on that account. The nineteenth-century reader preferred a different kind of story, one in which Dorothea Brooke is given a second chance, where Pip may lose his fairy gold but not, finally, his fairy princess. However fallen the hero—who ever seemed so irrecoverably lost as Raskolnikov, so suicidally adrift as Levin?—the possibility of a change of heart is an option forever available. Not until Hardy, heralding the harsher age to come, is a genuine plea for mercy rejected. Whether it be the theme of fruitful remorse that runs from Coleridge's Ancient Mariner to Wagner's Parsifal, or the theme of love triumphing over world and self that informs the major fiction of the time, somewhere in this literature, exultant or restrained, sounds the seraphic assurance of Dame Julian of Norwich: "Sin is behovely, but all shall be well and all shall be well and all manner of things shall be well."[2]

It had not always been thus. The change of heart so generously provided and so gratefully accepted by the Victorian sinner seems somehow denied to characters like Faustus, Macbeth, or Beatrice-Joanna in Thomas Middleton's *The Changeling*; the assurance that all shall be well is so cruelly inappropriate to the likes of Oedipus or Medea or Clytemnestra. The optimistic eschatology of Goethe's Faust and its legacy to nineteenth-century culture, so distant from the related outlooks of his predecessor, Marlowe, and his successor, Thomas Mann, have come to seem crass folly, a total misreading of life. Those who believe that man is inherently noble, with the gift of redemptive love forever at his disposal, have been increasingly forced onto the defensive in the face of modern iniquity. To act as defense counsel for man—precisely the impossible vocation forsaken by the enlightened "hero" of *The Fall*—seems fatuously quixotic in our time; tilting at windmills seems a far more rewarding activity.

Sartre turns modern disillusion into an advantage, something creditable, arguing that the hideous times through which we have lived have been educative, teaching us to take evil seriously, not merely as an appearance or as a privation, but as ontological reality; his conclusion will, he claims, "seem shocking to lofty souls: Evil cannot be redeemed."[3] This categorical assertion, with its tone of intimidatory, irrefutable discovery, is advanced as though Shakespeare had never created Iago nor Milton conceived the Satan of Mount Niphates; but, leaving aside the untenable claim to have unearthed a new, hitherto unapprehended truth, the assertion is clearly designed to rout forever the Pollyannaish daydreams of nineteenth-century liberals and the redemptive art of the preceding age.

Nor is it just an insistence that the doctrine of inherent goodness is a lie, a reminder that there is evil abroad as well as good, and that evil is real. As we read modern fiction, the fearful suspicion grows that evil, not goodness, is the ultimate reality, the truly strong thing, with Beelzebub lord of the world as well as the flies. *Amor vincit omnia*: some such assurance underwrites the confidence of the great nineteenth-century novelists, Dickens and George Eliot, Tolstoy and Dostoyevski. It is this assurance that is now at risk.

In Orwell's *Nineteen Eighty-four*, O'Brien, his tone that of a weary schoolmaster painfully instructing a perversely backward child, states, "You are under the impression that hatred is more exhausting than love. Why should it be?"[4] Winston's illusions, which prove so pitifully puerile, are that love is stronger than hatred, that good encompasses evil, that human nature has a bias toward goodness, that evil is a mere distraction, an error to be expunged, that in the long run all is for the best—precisely the axioms upon which nineteenth-century fiction is founded. Rebuking Winston for these childish misconceptions, O'Brien becomes a spokesman for twentieth-century "realism," putting the optimism of the earlier age in its puerile place. Winston is exposed to the same harsh but necessary education that Sartre claims as our dubious privilege: we have been badly taught but have now learned better. The link with *Lord of the Flies* is inescapable; the island is a schoolroom where the children, however brutally, learn to see life as it is and not as it is foolishly mediated through the Pollyannaish pages of a nineteenth-century romancer.

In this respect Golding's book is a representative text, at one with its epoch. The twentieth century has been a bad period for Pelagians, those who confidently proclaim the virtue and intelligence of human beings. Modern literature seems, on the whole, to support Augustine against Pelagius, emphasizing as it does the frailty and nastiness of men. When Adrian Leverkühn in Thomas Mann's *Doctor Faustus* announces his resolve to take back the *Ninth*, revoking what he sees as the fatuous lie of man's nobility as enshrined in the "Ode to Joy," he simultaneously announces the adversarial program of twentieth-century literature toward the work of its predecessor.[5] Today the promise is fulfilled—everything is taken back. Where was once salvation is now damnation; where love once ruled, there is the boot in the face forever. In place of the redeemed sinner, Carton and Dombey, Valjean and Raskolnikov, is the doomed criminal, Kurtz and Aschenbach. The creative remorse of Jean Valjean cedes to the sterile despair of Jean-Baptiste Clamence, "hero" of *The Fall* and baptist of our bitter dispensation. Instead of the serene assurance of Dame Julian, we hear the intimidating challenge at the close of *Lord of the Flies*, the more disconcerting because there seems to be no immediately plausible answer: who will save the officer and his ship, who will save *us*?

This is the dark epiphany: a realization of failure, futility, and sin, with no promise of reprieve or hope of redemption. "The absurd is sin without God": thus Camus identifies the peculiar torment of our predicament, its oxymoronic quality.[6] Without a judge who can absolve and redeem, we stand condemned forever: sin becomes agony, unbearable because remediless. We cannot forgive ourselves and there is no Atlas to take the weight of our sins on his shoulders. As desperately as Golding's Ralph, we need rescue, but there is no rescuer for us as there so luckily is for him. To explain the provenance of this dark epiphany, I shall investigate the relevance of *Gulliver's Travels* to our own cultural catastrophe. This text, written in the first quarter of the eighteenth century, provides a grid for locating our modern fictions, a template against which contemporary experience can be assessed and aligned. "The Voyage to the Houyhnhnms" is of special paradigmatic import; set against it, *Lord of the Flies* will assume a sharper definition and a deeper clarity.

In 1726 Swift issued a challenge to the Pelagianism of his day and supplied a model for Golding's onslaught against Victorian optimism. (The British fourth century monk Pelagius, in denying original sin, advanced a euphoric view of man's chances of salvation, which came close to rejecting the need for a redeemer—men could regain Eden through their own efforts and virtues.) Swift presented a bleaker view of man's condition, a view with certain affinities to our own contemporary variants of Augustinianism. (Saint Augustine's was a direly pessimistic view of the human condition—man was a vile creature, totally corrupted since the Fall and hence completely dependent for salvation on the gratuitous grace of a Saviour-God.) For following Augustine, Swift was rebuked, not by an enemy but by a friend, Lord Bolingbroke, his personal and political ally, who deplored the *Travels* on the ground that it was a bad design to depreciate human nature.[7] Man is basically good and is steadily becoming better; he is *animal rationale*, uniquely privileged among creatures as sharer in the divine gift of reason. It was, so Bolingbroke judged, scandalously offensive to besmirch the *imago dei* with the filth of the Yahoo. Even today, in our atrocity-benumbed century, Swift's book retains the power to unnerve, though Bolingbroke's sense of outrage at the insult to human nature understandably finds fewer seconders. Rather, the experience of Swift's alienated hero strikes us, in certain respects, as chillingly pertinent to that of certain key modern protagonists: to Marlow in *Heart of Dark-*

ness, detecting the fraud of western civilization in distant places; to Aschenbach in *Death in Venice*, bound on a journey that strangely merges self-discovery with self-destruction; to Orwell's broken wretch in *Nineteen Eighty-four*, learning that all his tenderly harbored delusions concerning truth, love, and freedom are mere brainwashing, reflexes mistaken for truth; to Golding's boys, as ineptly educated by their society as Gulliver is by his, discovering on the island that there is no refuge from corrupt civilization in Yahoo nature, no rescue in either city or jungle.

Certainly, *Gulliver's Travels* differs from modern manifestations of the dark epiphany, *Lord of the Flies* included, in one important respect: it comes before an age of optimism while they come after, marking the end of an era while they signal the emergence of a new sensibility. Swift's book is a last, brilliant Augustinian sortie against the armies of Enlightenment massing for the final assault upon the ruined fortress of seventeenth-century ideology. It was almost as if the expiring century had concentrated all its force in the person of Swift to launch one parting onslaught upon the deluded optimism of its successor.

As the *vous autres* letter to Pope and Bolingbroke shows, Swift believed that the new, optimistic view of man, built on the ruins of original sin, was dangerously mistaken (Swift, *Correspondence*, 3: 118). In the *Travels* he flung down the gauntlet to emergent, buoyant Pelagianism. The enemies he attacked were many and varied—deists, rationalists, freethinkers, philanthropists—but all were united in avowed or tacit denial of the doctrine of original sin and in a determination to absolve human nature of the charge of corruption. They were "the party of humanity," the task force resolved to deliver mankind from the shackles of Hobbes and Calvin alike.[8] Theology and philosophy had conspired to persuade men that they were fallen creatures, sinks of iniquity or selfish, treacherous animals whose very society was founded on fear and mistrust. It was long overdue for men to break the prison of original sin, renounce self-disparagement, and demand the restitution of the virtues stolen from them. On this, whatever other disagreements they had, the luminaries of the eighteenth-century Enlightenment were at one.

Against this meliorist tide, Swift stood like some Canute of Augustinianism. It is easy to see why his book incensed Bolingbroke and the party of humanity, that party to which the deluded Gulliver had belonged before his enlightenment by the rational horses. Swift took a very different view of man's estate from that of the philosophes. He found himself surrounded by men who thought themselves emancipated and were proud of their superiority—it was, for someone who never wondered to see men wicked, only to see them not ashamed,[9] like living among lepers who boasted of being sound: the claim, even more than the condition, provoked his contempt. He surveyed what the enlightened were pleased to call civilization with a scorn to match their complacency, because it was precisely the progressivist era that he regarded as degenerate. In the tradition of Old Testament pessimism, he was convinced that man was the vehicle of original sin and that his most flagrant offense was his insufferable pride in a false innocence:

> Their Deeds they all on Satan lay;
> The Devil did the Deed, not they.[10]

Swift despised the doublethink that permitted man to commit abominations while denying responsibility for them, to divorce existence from essence, to be one thing yet deem himself another. In our own time Reinhold Niebuhr expresses a similar puzzlement in the face of the same paradox: "No cumulation of contradictory evidence seems to disturb modern man's good opinion of himself. He considers himself the victim of corrupting institutions which he is about to destroy or reconstruct or the confusions of ignorance which an adequate education is about to overcome. Yet he continues to regard himself as essentially harmless and virtuous."[11] For Swift, as for Niebuhr, man's self-infatuation, his absorption in the myth of his own innocence, is his greatest transgression and worst affront. The myth of human goodness is Swift's prime target.

One by one he inspects the extolled institutions of European civilization—church, law, learning, science, government—to expose them as a sordid mixture of filth and folly. His book succeeded brilliantly in being offensive and wounding. Men who thought themselves innocent were convicted of guilt; men who boasted of being "rational creatures" were shown to be Yahoos; men unwarrantably happy were denied the right to be so. The chorus of protests from Bolingbroke onward makes plain that Swift's chief offense was to attack the myth of human goodness so dear to the liberal mentality, that mentality that was to secure its greatest triumph in the fiction of Victorian England. Swift despised this mentality as the product of pride and pursued it even when it took cover within traditional religion: "Miserable mortals! can we contribute to the glory of God?" (Swift, *Prose*, 9:263). Swift challenges the orthodox view expressed in the Anglican prayer book and taken to its extreme by certain theologians who argued that man, as God's creature, contributes to the creator's glory even in his damnation. It is a sign of Swift's vehemence against pride that he should distrust this Christian view as simply the old inveterate egotism wearing its Sunday clothes.

For him, not the luminous intellect but dark instincts govern man and society, and the sooner we admit this, the quicker we might do something about it. Parading as the friends of man, the philosophes are in truth his worst enemies, much as a quack who does not see a patient's illness threatens his life. "The Voyage to the Houyhnhnms" seeks to show the sufferer his true condition and to lash the charlatans who tell him he is well. Superficially a journey from Pelagius to Augustine, it is in reality from cozy domesticity to radical alienation, from an assumption of innocence to a conviction of sin.

Houyhnhnmland is at once education and disillusionment—the terms are virtually synonymous; Gulliver simultaneously stops being a fool, that is, a lover of humanity, and a happy man—happiness is the forfeit to experience. The truth sets him free but it is a bleak liberation. What he learns among the rational horses makes it impossible for him to continue as the good husband, father, and citizen who set out from home, but the happiness of these roles now appears as an Epicurean folly that the hero of truth must sternly forgo. He enters Houyhnhnmland well pleased with himself as Homo sapiens, *animal rationale*, the crown of creation; better still, he is European man, and, most conclusive of all, he is English man, the highest conceivable product of culture and the Everest of anthropological excellence. His implicit credo is that of a whole civilization at a moment of colonialist expansion, a civilization that regards its own superiority as axiomatic. It is this attitude that the experiences of the last voyage will radically subvert.

Gulliver is not brainwashed by the horses, as hostile critics, presumably still faithful lovers of humanity, sometimes allege. The brainwashing has occurred long before as a routine element of his English education: the unfaltering certitude that man is the perfection of nature, the unquestioned axiom of human superiority, the hubristic hauteur of the anthropomorphic delusion—man is Swift's quarry, not some subset of the species such as deists or freethinkers. Before the mind can entertain truth, it has to be cleared of cant; Gulliver must shed false learning first. The man who starts off expecting the horse to carry him ends up reverently stooping to kiss its hoof.

To protest that men are superior to horses is to blunder into the trap—we knew that before Houyhnhnmland. We accompany Gulliver to Houyhnhnmland to have our certitudes shaken, forsaking the assumptions that flatter us, confronting our true condition. One of the chief aims of the *Travels* is to show that we live in perceptual prisons, slaves to arbitrary norms elevated to the status of axioms, forever mistaking mere custom for cognition, conditioning for truth. "The Voyage to the Houyhnhnms" is at once an education in truth and guilt. We proceed through the charge sheet until every institution to which we pointed in proof of our virtue is exposed as a filthy sham. What Gulliver learns is that the dear place of his nativity is a sewer, his continent a cesspool. Denied asylum, driven back to the sewer, he writes his *Travels*, not to divert but to mortify his fellow Yahoos. The trial of Gulliver hinges on a question of identity, with the mirrors of Houyhnhnmland, the pools of water, reflecting the painful truth: when Gulliver stares into them, he sees staring back the face of the Yahoo. It is the final lesson in Gulliver's curriculum, the dark epiphany toward which the whole voyage moves. After all his travels, Gulliver discovers himself.

The genius to shock and dismay; the journey from spurious goodness to appalling truth; the dark epiphany in which the self is compelled, through a radical dislocation of experience, to confess aspects of its own nature formerly suppressed or ignored: all this makes Swift's masterpiece the ideal paradigm for assessing the dark works of our time, foremost among these being *Lord of the Flies*.

Golding's novel recapitulates in a fable immediately resonant to a twentieth-century sensibility the themes that originate in Swift: the dread that civilization is simply a veneer over bestiality; that the self is merely the fragile product of a particular conditioning that alters unnervingly with the altered matrix; that orgiastic surrender to a dark irrationalism is always a temptation and sometimes a fate; that we are shockingly obliged to give psychological houseroom to strangers who claim kinship, to Yahoo and sadist, both of whom disconcertingly seem to have equal residential rights with our more decorous, flattering selves. In its final memorable scene, Golding's book supplies us with one of the most strikingly explicit renditions of the dark epiphany in modern literature, when the newly rescued Ralph, to the embarrassed incomprehension of his superficial savior, weeps for the end of innocence and the darkness of man's heart. That Swift remains to the end a great comedian while Golding favors tragedy should not disguise the similarity of their disclosures.

Golding, as much as his book, seems the fitting terminus for an investigation of Gulliver's legacy. If, in fulfillment of Leverkühn's vow in *Doctor Faustus*, the twentieth century has pursued a policy of revocation toward the work of its predecessor, it is Golding who has proved the most overt and deliberate of revokers. Almost all of his early work is a taking back, a rescinding of certain long-established views and idees reçues (conventional wisdom). His second novel, *The Inheritors*, sets out to invalidate the optimistic view of human development held by H. G. Wells; its epigraph is provided by *The Outline of History* in which Wells celebrates the coming of Homo sapiens and his victory over Neanderthal man. Wells presents the latter as a half-witted, bloodthirsty creature, prototype of the cannibalistic ogre of folk-tale, while his supplanter is shown as thoughtful and resourceful, fit ancestor of our superior selves. Even more pertinent to the plot of Golding's book is Wells's short story "The Grisly Folk," in which the Neanderthal monsters steal a human child and are then, with Wells's complete approval, hunted down and destroyed by the new men in an act at once retributive and progressive. *The Inheritors* stands Wells on his head by depicting the Neanderthals as gentle and innocent, the newcomers as vicious and aggressive. (To this day man still believes that progress and the extermination of his enemies are the same thing.) For Golding it is man who ruins the garden by introducing evil into it; the serpent is redundant in his revision of Genesis—no more than Swift will he allow the devil to be made a scapegoat for human sins.

His third novel, *Pincher Martin*, does to *Robinson Crusoe* as a myth of human fortitude what *The Inheritors* does to "The Grisly Folk," and is equally outrageous in the reversal it proposes. From Prometheus onward we have come, through culture and inclination alike, to cherish the hero who, rejecting capitulation or despair, pits his unsustained, unconquerable self against the overwhelming tyranny of external circumstance. How can we withhold admiration from these champions of the self who cry no surrender even to inexorable reality? Pincher, clinging to his ocean rock after being torpedoed, seems for much of the book to be yet another irresistible candidate for heroic apotheosis, a worthy son of Prometheus; only gradually do we become aware that another, very different view of the situation is being pressed upon us. A series of flashbacks reveals a nasty, competitive person, bent on self-gratification even if it means destroying others. The snarling man, defying sea and sky, involved in his fierce and cunning appetite to survive, is simply exhibiting the same thralldom to appetite, the same wicked infatuation with his precious self, that caused so much agony to others before his shipwreck. Pincher is not a hero but a damned soul. We learn that he has, in fact, been dead from the first page and that the speciously heroic stand against the self's extinction is, properly understood, a timid, childish refusal to face the truth. What we have deludedly prized as our noblest quality is revealed as a sordid bondage, making us a woe unto ourselves and a menace to others.

But it is his first and best-known novel, *Lord of the Flies*, that reveals Golding as the supreme revoker, the most open abrogator in modern literature, employing the dark discoveries of our century to disclaim the vapid innocence of its predecessor. The obvious target is R. M. Ballantyne's boys' adventure story *The Coral Island*. Far from attempting to conceal his creative "theft," Golding points up the ironic contrast by lifting even the names of the boys from the earlier work. Ballantyne's book is important less as literature than as a document in the history of ideas, reflecting as it does a Victorian euphoria, a conviction that the world is a rational place where problems arise so that sensible, decent men can solve them. God has his place in this world, but his adversary is pleasingly absent and, with him, the sin that is his hold on humanity. The Home Counties come to the jungle and win easily. Difficulties are confidently and cheerfully overcome; fire is acquired easily and safely, pigs are hunted and killed without guilt or bloodshed. The only troublesome things—cannibals and pirates—come from outside and are bested by British grit and common sense. What cannibal is so foolish as to eat human flesh in preference to pig? All he needs is the proper culinary advice, and Ballantyne knows the boys to give it. They, for their part, know nothing of Beelzebub: they are godly, cleanly, sensible, decent, and efficient, and their island adventure is a kind of initiative test providing gratifying proof that they are just about ready to assume the blessed work of extending the British Empire throughout the savage world.

> Get you the sons your father got,
> And God will save the Queen.[12]

The braggadocio of Housman's words is anticipated in Ballantyne's hosanna of self-congratulation: the Coral Island boys are the sons of their proud fathers and the civilized values of the *pax Britannica* are guaranteed so long as such progeny persists.

Lord of the Flies was conceived in a radically different moral landscape, and Golding himself tells us that the horrors of World War II were crucial in producing this alteration. When Sammy Mountjoy, the hero of *Free Fall*, remarks that "the supply of nineteenth-century optimism and goodness had run out before it reached me," and goes on to describe the world as "a savage place in which man was trapped without hope," one senses an authorial reinforcement behind the words.[13] The last quotation might well serve as synopsis for *Lord of the Flies*. The book springs from the catastrophe of our time and not, as has been foolishly alleged, from the petty rancor of an arts graduate peeved because today the scientists have all the posts and prestige (Martin Green; 454). To attribute the book to a sullen distaste for the contemporary world, to depict Golding as another Jack who, when he can't have his own way, won't play any more and goes off in a huff, all because the scientist has displaced the literary intellectual as leader of society, is dignified by describing it as a *niaiserie* (derisively foolish idea).

But such criticism does at least have the merit of focusing attention on Golding's attitude toward science. He had started to read science at university on the twin assumptions that "science was busy cleaning up the universe" and that "there was no place in this exquisitely logical universe for the terrors of darkness" (*Hot Gates*, 172)—recognizable as a more sophisticated version of the vain assurance that Piggy attempts to provide in the text, and enough, surely, to give pause to those critics who identify Piggy as the book's hero. For the darkness stubbornly refused to scatter and Golding came to suspect (as Bertrand Russell likewise did, tutored by book 3 of *Gulliver's Travels*)[14] that science is not the savior, but, in the wrong hands, might well become our ruin. When Jack steals Piggy's glasses and becomes the thief of fire, he uses the stolen technology to intensify the nightmare, finally setting the island ablaze. H. G. Wells notwithstanding, bad men can be good scientists—only a scientific fideist will insist that science has a monopoly on virtue, a blunder long since exposed by Swift's Giant King. For Golding the war confirmed that "the darkness was all around, inexplicable, unexorcised, haunted, a gulf across which the ladder (science) lay without reaching the light" (*Hot Gates*, 174). Allowing for the heightened mode of expression, this is much the same pessimistic perception as Freud's toward the previous war, and no one, surely, is going to accuse Freud of being a disgruntled arts graduate envious of the scientists' acclaim.[15]

Golding's explanation of how his book came to be written seems far more convincing: "I set out to discover whether there is that in man which makes him do what he does, that's all. . . . [T]he Marxists are the only people left who think humanity is perfectible. But I went through the War and that changed me. The War taught me different and a lot of others like me."[16] This echoes Sartre's remark about our education in evil, with the war doing for Golding what Room 101 does for Winston Smith and what the island finally does for Ralph: providing the harsh but welcome corrective to a foolishly optimistic education. Among the lessons learned was that Ballantyne was retailing illusions—namely, that man is basically noble, that reason must prevail over darkness, that science is the prerogative of the civilized man.

The key to *Lord of the Flies* is in Golding's words—"that *in* man which makes him do what he does" (emphasis added). He will not permit blame to be attributed to the environment; the island is not responsible for what happens to the boys. His book is a challenge to Rousseau, "an attempt to trace the defects of society back to the defects of human nature. Before the war, most Europeans believed that man could be perfected by perfecting his society. We saw a hell of a lot in the war that can't be accounted for except on the basis of original evil."[17] It is the doctrine against which Swift's enemies, the philosophes, had fulminated so fiercely, the doctrine rehabilitated by the hideous events of twentieth-century history. Orwell's nightmare is a boot in the face forever, a world devoted to cruelty for its own sake, Roger's paradise. Camus in *The Fall* invites us to ponder the little-ease and the spitting-cell, the first an ingenious medieval invention, the second the equally masterly contrivance of the most advanced nation in modern Europe.[18] Had the rescuing officer not arrived, the boys would doubtless have contrived to create their own equivalent of these infernal machines.

Golding makes his own notable contribution to the tradition of the dark epiphany as he seeks to discover "that in man which makes him do what he does," anatomizing these juvenile replicas of Shakespeare's Regan to see what breeds about their hearts. It is no diminution of the power and originality of *Lord of the Flies* to insist that it is not so isolated from any mainstream of speculation, as is sometimes suggested, for Golding shares a certain sensibility with other key writers of our age, such as Orwell and Camus, with all claiming a common literary father in the Swift of *Gulliver's Travels*. To dismiss these men as mere malcontents, a literary Cave of Adullam, a gang of petulant and disaffected litterateurs miffed at a scientific takeover, is as foolish as it is impertinent.

Golding has perhaps connived at his own depreciation by describing himself as a parodist and parody as depending on the mean advantage of being wise after someone else's event.[19] There is no intention here of presenting *Lord of the Flies* as parasitic upon *Gulliver's Travels*, no question of any mean advantage being taken of that great event, far less of that immeasurably lesser event, *The Coral Island*. Golding is guilty of a similarly ungenerous self-devaluation in referring to himself as a pint-size Jeremiah, almost as though he were colluding with those who dismiss him as a peddler of doom—content, perhaps even elated, to describe the ruins around us.[20] To deride oneself for being able to read the signs of the times and, greater feat still, to shape that reading into a fable of such power and originality as *Lord of the Flies*, is an injustice against which the reader must protest. Part of the greatness of *Gulliver's Travels* is, one must remark, its prophetic element, its adversarial heroism, as Swift single-handedly challenges the complacency of his age—the pride of the philosophes was the wave of the future. Golding, by contrast, wrote his book after the fall, a fall that even the party of humanity could not deny. When H. G. Wells issues as his dying testament *Mind at the End of Its Tether*, one may safely conclude that the jig is up for nineteenth-century doctrines of progress.

But there is no shame in correcting the errors of a discredited orthodoxy, and it is misleading of Golding or anyone else to speak as though *Lord of the Flies* were merely an inversion of *The Coral Island*, a realistic retelling of an exploded fantasy. Golding is most interesting when he is most creative, when he deserts parody altogether. Just as *Joseph Andrews* becomes a comic masterpiece when Fielding leaves off burlesquing Richardson and liberates his own imagination, so the real triumph of *Lord of the Flies* is not its parodic demolition of Ballantyne but the innovative skill that is most strikingly evident in the creation of Piggy, Simon, and Roger—a skill without precedent in the earlier book. This is what makes it an original work of art, the authentic expression of its age, not simply a spoof deriving its second-hand force from the work of another era. How sin enters the garden: it is, after all, the oldest story in Western culture and Golding's contemporary rendition is a worthy continuation of the tradition.

In assessing the influence of *Gulliver's Travels* upon *Lord of the Flies*, our discriminations must be altogether finer, more delicately precise. *The Coral Island* is too slight a text to be in any but the most superficial way commensurate with the work so often unjustly limited as its parody. To think of *The Coral Island* as giving birth to *Lord of the Flies* is like attributing the paternity of a giant to a pygmy. The *Travels* is a very different matter. Ballantyne's fantasy of island life is so adrift from the world known to Golding that all he had to do to expose it was to include the elements so decorously ignored by the Victorian writer—dirt, diarrhea, hysteria, bloodlust, the excrement on the fruit, the stake up the sow's anus, Simon's body on the beach, Piggy's brains on the rock—all those aspects of dark, disgusting nature from which Ballantyne studiously averted his gaze. Where better to acquire these missing elements than from the great master of disgust, Jonathan Swift? How more devastatingly expose Ballantyne's blunders than by contrasting the island experience of his boys with the very different island experience of Lemuel Gulliver? In particular, Swift could be recruited to attack the opposing delusions of two groups with whom Golding wished to quarrel: those who recommend a retreat to nature from the decadence of civilization and those who uphold society as a shield against the savagery of nature.

It has long been recognized that Swift is the master of entrapment, forever luring the baffled reader into impasse and stalemate. The most celebrated of such deadlocks in his work is the "Digression on Madness," with its bewildering antitheses of sunny surface and dark interior, mindless hedonism and stricken insight, which leave the reader desperately treading air, seeking in vain a toehold upon certitude, a precious square of unassailable footage.[21] In vain, because Swift deliberately induces a sense of disorientation, shattering the trust he invites, exulting in the havoc he provokes: "I damn such Fools! Go, go, you're bit" (Swiftly, *Poems*, 2:579). Swift's is an art hostile to the reader, never more so than when he is treacherously addressed as "gentle reader"; betrayal is Swift's business.

The last book of the *Travels* is such a trap, leaving the reader stranded like Bouridan's ass between the equally unacceptable alternatives of nature and culture: fleeing the filth of the one, he falls into the filth of the other. Gulliver is forced to concede that the Yahoo is natural man, stripped of all the reinforcements of culture and the amenities of society. It is the culmination of Lear's act of divestment on the health when all the "lendings" have been scattered to the winds, and only the poor, forked animal remains. It is to this creature that Swift gives the name Yahoo. We are not, clearly, to seek salvation in nature.

But neither, in the *Travels*, are we to turn to society, to civilization, as a refuge from nature. To protest that we are not Yahoos but civilized Europeans will not serve in this text. The whole purpose of Gulliver's Houyhnhnm education is to show how deceptive is the apparent division between Yahoo and European, savagery and civilization, and to impress that there is no escape from nature into culture. Europe is simply Yahoodom triumphant, because when there is no pest-control, the pests may do as they please. The sophisticated nastiness of Europe is even more noxious, since there are no rational horses to keep the vermin in check. How terrible it would be, reflects the Houyhnhnm Master, if there existed anywhere an animal as vile as the Yahoo but equipped with the brainpower so fortunately denied that loathsome creature (294). In Europe the appalled supposition is fact: the "civilized" Yahoo combines the savagery of a beast with the technology of an ingenious psychopath. If nature in the Yahoo is vile, reason in the European is worse, simply making natural malice the more lethal—lack of claws or talons is no handicap to the inventor of gunpowder. On fallacious Houyhnhnm premises, man, so blessedly disabled, has no hope of ever becoming the master animal that the myth of Eden makes him: lord of the garden, creation his fiefdom. Golding follows Swift in showing the disastrous results of God's decision to elect man to this high office. Liberated from rational horses or disciplining adults, Yahoo men and Yahoo boys (there is merely a trivial difference in size) ruin the garden and forfeit paradise. However we turn in Swift and Golding alike, toward nature or society, we confront the same nightmare, in primitive or refined form. There is no remedy in the *Travels*, simply a sense of impasse and a final insulting dismissal of man as a creature beyond redemption.

What is still to be adequately recognized is the extent to which *Lord of the Flies* replicates the ground plan of *Gulliver's Travels*, unearthing the same discoveries, climaxing in an analogous impasse. Both texts compel us to scrutinize anew those slothful assumptions we so carelessly take for knowledge. Who are the savages in Gulliver's last voyage—those who try to kill him with poisoned arrows or those in Portugal who, if they heard his story, would burn him in the fires of the Inquisition? (337). Officially, the former are savages, the latter civilized. Swift asks if we are happy with this demarcation. In *Lord of the Flies* Golding shows us a boy with a stick and a man with a nuclear warship and asks us to say which is the greater threat to life. Yet we still have so much irrelevant labor expended on arguments as to whether *Lord of the Flies* is a "tory" text, an implicit tribute to the salutary disciplines of society, bereft of which, men must lapse into ruinous anarchy. To see Golding as the heir of Swift would prevent such misguided industry, for no more than his master does Golding promise salvation in the city or declare that only in the jungle are we at risk. Nature is as much a metaphor in Golding as in Bunyan. When Ralph laments "the wearisomeness of this life, where every path was an improvisation and a considerable part of one's waking life was spent watching one's feet" (83), his immediate reference is, of course, to the literal difficulty of walking in the jungle, but the wider, metaphorical implications are unmistakable. It would be as foolish to believe that fear and frustration are confined to the tropics as to take the Slough of Despond for a criticism of the local roads authority. As much as Swift, Golding denies the segregation of jungle and home countries; the problems are the same, merely transposed to a new setting and wearing a different vestment. That is the meaning of that concluding parallax when the rescuing officer arrives and the perspective is so startlingly altered. Here, too, Gulliver's legacy is evident, for Swift reveals himself in Lilliput and Brobdingnag as the master of perspective, and Golding proves an exemplary pupil in his own virtuoso performance throughout his book.

The parallels multiply on inspection. Islands are ideal for such fictions, providing the perfect laboratory conditions—hermetic, remote, fenced off from irrelevance—for the testing of human nature. Gulliver protests the irrelevance of his writings to affairs at home: how could events so distant be applicable to the state of England? (37–38). Golding's adventure story has a parallel deceptiveness. What have the actions of a bunch of boys stranded on an island to do with us, except to provide a pleasant way of passing our time? Yet Golding as much as Gulliver writes for our amendment, not our entertainment. These travels abroad disclose the truth of home. Gulliver is soon indignantly demanding how any reader dare question the authenticity of the Yahoos when they abound in London and Dublin—admittedly wearing clothes and using a jabber of language, but undeniably Yahoos for all that (40). One recalls how American publishers initially rejected *Animal Farm* on the ground that there was no market for animal stories. *Lord of the Flies* is a boys' adventure story in the sense that *Animal Farm* is an animal story or *Gulliver's Travels* a piece of travel literature. Behind the facade of all three is a warning and an exhortation: attention must be paid, for it is a matter of salvation. *Lord of the Flies* is only ostensibly about the rescue of Ralph; much more pertinent and taxing is the problem of the rescuer's rescue, the salvation of the savior. This is the real problem of the text, insoluble within its pages, pressing upon the book's readers: here the author makes no claim to authority. In this challenge to the reader (audible, surely, even without the prompting of Golding's extratextual tuition),[22] the text links up with contemporary works like *The Fall* and *Nineteen Eighty-four*, all manifestly derivative of *Gulliver's Travels*. Is it necessary to repeat that to use "derivative" in such a context is the highest compliment that one can pay?

There are, undeniably, important differences between Swift and Golding. Swift always begins in normalcy, with Gulliver at home and all well before setting out on his next strange adventure. He is rooted in the mundane, a family man with the customary obligations before his metamorphosis into giant or manikin, observer of zany theoreticians or celebrant of Houyhnhnm virtues. This anchorage in banal reality certifies the authenticity of his adventures; so unremarkable a man patently lacks the imagination to concoct such tales. By contrast,

Swift's pupils, Orwell and Golding, call immediate attention to the strangeness of the situation: something is demonstrably amiss when a clock ominously strikes thirteen at the opening of *Nineteen Eighty-four* or when a boy in school uniform is found clambering through the creepers of a tropical jungle—crisis is already upon us. Instead of the circumstantial detail that Gulliver so dutifully supplies, there is a curious reticence in *Lord of the Flies* as to the background of the children, and this dearth of information is revelatory of what Golding chose to reject in writing his novel. We learn that Piggy's father is dead and that he was brought up by an aunt who kept a sweetshop, that Ralph's father is a naval officer who taught his son to swim when he was five. But the whereabouts, even the very existence, of their mothers remains a mystery; to the end we do not know if they are motherless through death, divorce, or abandonment. We know nothing at all of the kind of homes that produced Jack or Roger or Simon. The most circumstantial piece of information supplied—the address and telephone number of Percy Weyms Madison—is completely trivial, of no value to the reader or, finally, to the near-demented boy himself: it has lost its talismanic charm and become mere gibberish, a chant without import, before fading from memory altogether. Golding's disdain for the circumstantial detail of conventional realistic fiction underlines such neglect; all he needs is a group of children on a desert island and a minimum of information about their former lives—that Jack sang high C and once led a choir is all we need to know to follow his development. Golding as author is almost as secretive as Roger as character.

Despite these differences, *Lord of the Flies* and *Gulliver's Travels* share a common aim and origin in their creators' resolve to shatter the myth of innocence, and the earlier work supplies a shape as well as an impetus, a map for traversing the same route from optimism to despair. As Gulliver is driven to acknowledge himself Yahoo, so the boys are forced to confess the presence of the beast within, dwelling not in the forest but in the darkness of the human heart: parallel recognitions.

General ground plan apart, there are more detailed reverberations of Swift in Golding's text, such as the views on government and the theme of deterioration. Swift's detestation of the whole *arcana imperii* tradition of government, the idea that the art of ruling is an elitist skill denied to the multitude, recurs in Ralph's dismay at the practiced debaters, Piggy included, who use their gifts to sophisticate truth and twist the meetings. We read in Swift that "Providence never intended to make the management of public affairs a mystery," and the exemplary Giant King despises all refinement in what is, after all, a matter of

applied commonsense (176). The idiom is not Ralph's, but the senti-
ments are. The first assembly meets in a mood of buoyant democracy,
the right to speak and be heard, even for a littlun, symbolized in the
conch: everyone can be a legislator. From the outset Jack holds an
opposing, elitist view: only the few are entitled to speak and govern—
by the close, this has narrowed down to himself alone. After the initial
euphoria, Ralph is increasingly baffled at how difficult governing is,
and his resentment against the devious rhetoricians for complicating
what should be simple and straightforward—the paramountcy of rescue, hence the need for a signal fire—echoes the anger of the Giant
King. Recalling Gulliver's eulogistic account of the Houyhnhnm assembly—"controversies, wranglings, disputes, and positiveness in false
or dubious propositions are evils unknown among the Houyhnhnms"
(315)—and contrasting this with the bad-tempered, illogical, disputa-
tious assemblies of *Lord of the Flies*, one must conclude that the boys
are not rational creatures in Gulliver's sense.

Deterioration is also present in both texts in theme and structure
alike. Gulliver is shipwrecked by a storm, abandoned by companions
intent on saving themselves, captured by pirates and set adrift in an
open boat through the malice of a fellow Christian, and finally betrayed by a mutiny of his own crew. His successive adventures record
a transition from purely natural disaster through human frailty to the
blackest of human deeds, spite and treachery. The movement is one
of deepening evil. The process of internalizing evil and giving it human
features culminates when Gulliver, embraced by the she-Yahoo, acknowledges his kinship in a corruption not monopolized by pirates
and mutineers.

A parallel retrogression from accident to evil occurs in *Lord of
the Flies*. No blame attaches to the boys for being marooned on the
island; they are the innocent victims of a nuclear war that their fathers—the adults for whom Piggy has such unwarrantable respect—
started. But thereafter the fall from innocence is swift and irreversible,
as the boys show themselves to be their fathers' sons. The first death,
that of the child with the birthmark, is an accident, caused at worst
by carelessness. Exuberant at the hope of rescue, the boys rush to light
a fire, and, in their undisciplined folly, the fire gets out of control and
the child is burned. Yet their intention is good, they mean well—
failure is one of intelligence, not of will. They should have known
better, been more circumspect: this is the limit of liability. After this,
however, it is downhill all the way. When Simon dies, it is not physical
nature but human nature that rages out of control. Maddened by fear
and savage, atavistic ritual, the demented mob kills the boy as he

staggers out of the forest in the nightmarish delusion that he is the beast. It is a frenzied slaughter, as mindless as that in *The Bacchae* when the king's mother unwittingly leads the horde that tears her son to pieces. In both cases guilt is partially mitigated by possession, a madness that the mind cannot resist. "Forgive them, for they know not what they do": the words of the dying Jesus might generously be extended to the Bacchic women and Golding's boys alike.

No such palliation is possible when Piggy, blind and helpless, clinging terrified to the narrow ledge, is smashed to pieces by the huge rock released by Roger. It is with a sense of delirious abandonment that Roger willingly, indeed eagerly, succumbs to a lust to kill. He knows what he's doing and wants to do it; he has cosseted and cultivated his obsession—for him the universe holds no greater delight than another's pain. Jack, too, knows what he is doing when, "viciously, with full intention," he hurls the spear at Ralph and then plans a hunt—signals, strategy, and all, to catch and kill his enemy (200). The stick sharpened at both ends becomes the chilling objective correlative of the evil within Roger and Jack, proving the truth of Simon's intuition that the beast is at home in men. Vainly, Ralph tries to delude himself that the deterioration is mere mishap, the fall into evil unwilled and accidental, echoing the Socratic argument that no man does evil knowingly—there is no wickedness, only error. Evil as deliberate choice seems too bad to be possible. (Arthur Miller speaks of our modern inability to conceive a Iago, someone devoted to evil for its own sake: "Evil, be thou my good," in the oxymoron of Milton's Satan.[23]) Ralph's liberal mind shies away from such lucid, open-eyed evil, until "the fatal unreasoning knowledge" forces itself upon him: "These painted savages would go further and further" (203); the logic of the Fall is that it stops only in hell. But for the officer's intervention, Ralph would have suffered the fate of a pig—his head left for the lord of the flies, his carcass roasted and eaten by the hunters. In Ballantyne the boys convert the cannibals; in Golding they are about to become them. From carelessness to frenzy to murderous impulse to a planned dedication to evil: the descent into hell in *Lord of the Flies* is as visible as it is in Dante.

There are, as the final chapter of this study shows, major differences in Golding's and Swift's attitudes toward nature; Golding frequently matches Swift's disgust, but never in Swift do we encounter that ecstatic celebration of natural beauty that occasionally illuminates the pages of Golding's text. Yet, balancing this in Golding is an excremental vision as obtrusive as anything in Swift. "I shit on your heaven," screams Pincher Martin to God,[24] and some critics mistakenly trace in the preoccupation with excrement a sign of the author's Manichaean aversion to physical life, a revulsion from man as excrement, disturbingly reminiscent of Swift's scatological poems. The preoccupation is certainly there. *Lord of the Flies* opens with diarrhea, with Piggy's bowel movements commanding attention in much the same way as Gulliver's. Our first view of Piggy is from the rear; only afterward do we see his glasses. Within seconds he is a bespectacled excreter, grunting like an animal as he crouches to defecate. The first responder to the conch is a littlun who steps out of soiled shorts as he moves toward the strange sound (18–19). Golding follows Swift in compelling us to confront the inescapable filth that we produce but conceal or pretend does not exist. In Lilliput Gulliver's evacuations are a major pollution problem, in Brobdingnag a recurring source of embarrassment for the hero. From Piggy's opening spasms, the subject recurs throughout *Lord of the Flies*. Ralph is forced to warn the littluns against excreting too near the fruit trees—filthy man polluting his environment (87). Simon's mysterious nocturnal movements are coarsely and erroneously ascribed by Jack to his being "caught short" (93); and when Simon struggles to enlighten his companions by asking them to think of the nastiest thing there is, Jack once again—significantly, to howls of laughter—answers with Pincher Martin's word (97). Our shame finds relief in laughter and Simon discovers how difficult it is to instruct the willfully deaf and the culpably vulgar. Nor is Jack altogether wrong, his coarse obtuseness notwithstanding: beast and excrement alike come from within. We turn food into energy and excrement—the first dangerous, the other dirty—and Golding finds the fitting symbol for both activities in the Lord of the Flies, who is also the Lord of Dung. If man is excrement, here is his master.

Nevertheless, it remains true for Golding (though perhaps less so for Swift) that the nature held up for judgment is the moral nature of human beings rather than physical nature itself, whether external world or human body. The rats that recur in Swift and his pupil, Orwell, are absent in Golding. Gulliver is threatened, Winston destroyed, by rats—by nature at its most loathsome. There are no noxious animals in *Lord of the Flies*, because human nature is Golding's prime concern. In Genesis the snake—another loathsome creature, like the rat—enters Eden to ruin man: no serpent, no Fall. In *Lord of the Flies*, by contrast, the snake is a figment of the human imagination, a fiction bred by disordered dreams. The boys need no literal serpent to tempt them, no rats to demoralize and break them; Golding presents a do-it-yourself temptation whereby the boys corrupt themselves and unilaterally ruin Eden. There is no serious external threat in *Lord of the Flies*, nothing remotely resembling Orwell's Room 101. There are problems, certainly—intense heat, storm, rain, darkness—but none so taxing that it cannot be solved, as Winston Smith so pitifully cannot solve his.

Despite Swift's disgust with certain aspects of physical life, the problem for Gulliver among the Houyhnhnms is never an economic problem, a test of physical survival. Houyhnhnmland is a paradise where Gulliver discovers "how easily nature is satisfied," and declares, "I never had one hour's sickness, while I stayed in this island" (279). Whatever catastrophe occurs, nature and environment are exonerated. Unlike Crusoe, Gulliver need not battle just to stay alive; for him, human nature is the threat—not his environment but his self. The same is true of Golding's castaways, as Simon's startling interruption makes plain: "as if it wasn't a good island" (56). He clearly believes that it is, and the other boys pay tribute to the island's bounty. Fresh water, fruit, and meat are all in plentiful supply. Survival is relatively easy; they need only build shelters and keep a signal fire going. Ralph regards it as a piece of cake and is, in a sense, right. It is almost as if Golding set out to rebut Aldous Huxley's attack on Wordsworth for taking the Lake District as a representative sample of nature's kindness—born in jungle or desert, he might, so Huxley alleged, have thought otherwise.[25] Although Golding's boys live in the tropics, he is resolved that nature shall not be made scapegoat for their misdeeds—no more than that society should take the rap for the crimes of civilized men. Externally, the boys have all they need to survive; it is their internal resources that are inadequate.

Boys who abuse nature, foolishly destroying their supply of wood at the start, wantonly incinerating the island at the close, have no cause to blame nature—it is the fire makers who are to blame for the fire. Their true battle is with themselves; it is never economic in the crude Marxist sense. Simon as prophet assures his companions that the island is good and that there is no snake in the forest. The snake is the product of bad dreams, belonging to the same order of existence as Macbeth's bloodstained dagger: how do you purge the mind? The beast is not real, but evil is, because human beings produce it as bees produce honey (*Hot Gates*, 87). It is significant that the only "rotten" place on the good island is the place that Jack instantaneously falls in love with—Castle Rock, over which he almost drools: so ideal for a fort, so perfect for hurling boulders on a foe beneath (116). It is not nature's fault if Jack has an evil mind, if he wants a totally unnecessary fort, if he loves forts for their own sake and will always be able to create the enemies to justify them. It would be absurd to blame the boulder for killing Piggy and not the boy who launched it. As determinedly as Swift, Golding sets his face against exculpation or alibi, resolved to expose human nature as the culprit, refuting Rousseau by tracking the defects of society to the defects of the individual rather than making society the scapegoat for our sins. Not society, nor nature, nor Beelzebub himself is to blame, for the Lord of the Flies has power only over those who commit themselves to his service.

Hence the importance of individual responsibility and self-knowledge. Know thyself: not the mastery of external nature but a true acquaintance with the self—the highest aspiration of pagan wisdom—is also the aim of *Gulliver's Travels* and *Lord of the Flies*. There is no guarantee that self-knowledge will promote self-esteem; education may lead to awareness of guilt. "There were few greater lovers of mankind, at that time, than myself," Gulliver says, referring to his ignorant, pre-Houyhnhnm self, in love with his own and mankind's innocence (277). Yet, Niebuhr reminds us that the myth of innocence can easily consort with mass murder, as Eichmann in Jerusalem so strikingly illustrates. Gulliver's stay among the horses is the record of an education, a revaluation, a complete re-vision. Ralph experiences a similar reeducation, and his final breakdown testifies to the severity of the instruction.

"He was wholly at a loss to know what could be the use or necessity of practising those vices": The Houyhnhnm Master's bafflement at human evil (290) is shared by Ralph anguishing over Jack's misdeeds, despite the fact that at certain crucial moments (the "mock" beating of Robert, the horrific killing of Simon) he himself joins in. The element of self-incrimination is mandatory in the tradition of the dark epiphany: the fall of man, not the indictment of one's enemies, is its theme. It is because Piggy can see only the sins of the other, not his own, that he fails to be the hero of such a tradition. On the hilltop the boys see "something like a great ape," and flee in terror from it (136). It is the most serious mistake, the most startling moment of nonrecognition, in the book, since it is the dead parachutist, human like themselves, whom they fail to identify. Gulliver, too, first sees the Yahoo as alien and repulsive, completely unrelated to himself—but he learns better. The chief aim of education should be knowledge of the self, not mastery of the world. What doth it profit a man to gain the world and lose his soul? What doth it profit a man to know the world and not himself?

The most egregious instance of self-ignorance is exhibited in Piggy, champion of common sense. After the murder of Simon, in his frantic search for a "formula" (173)—the scientific term is significant—that will preserve his innocence (in consummate confirmation of Niebuhr's paradox), Piggy, angrily rebuking Ralph, denies that *he* is a murderer. Simon's death is, he claims, an act without an agent, a deed without a doer, or else—Piggy at his most concessive—the atrocity must be extenuated, forgiven or ignored. There is a fascinating depiction of the alibi-fabricating animal detested by Swift ("The Devil did the Deed, not they") as Piggy shifts through the hopelessly contradictory stages of his defense (172–75). Simon is dead and no amount of talk can bring him back—best to forget and put it all behind. Fear was to blame—the darkness, the storm, the dance; not Piggy's true self but some uncontrollable usurper tore Simon to death. Simon is not dead at all but only pretending; there was no murder. Piggy did not fully participate, because, half-blind, he could not see what was happening. Piggy did not participate at all, for he was outside the circle. What happened was pure accident, in our blasphemous jargon an act of God for which no one should be blamed; there is a corpse but no murder—the argument of Dmitry's trendy, liberal lawyer in *The Brothers Karamazov*. The victim was to blame; the batty boy, irresponsibly crawling out of the dark, "asked for it" (173); the murderers are guiltless, while the corpse is arraigned. Finally, this straggle of confused alibis, each destined like the priests of some savage rite to kill its predecessor, fumbles its way back to amnesia as the remedy: "We got to forget this. We can't do no good thinking about it, see?" (173). For once the morality is as shoddy as the grammar. Swift, one feels, would have approved this revelation of man as the animal that sins and denies guilt.

Piggy, his protestations notwithstanding, has fallen with the others. The Fall is at the heart of these two texts, separated from each other by more than two centuries. From Genesis onward, the Fall has been somehow linked with sexuality, and in *Gulliver's Travels* and *Lord of the Flies* alike, the sexual test provides the decisive proof of corruption. When the female Yahoo leaps lasciviously upon Gulliver, identification is irrefutably confirmed: "For now I could no longer deny, that I was a real Yahoo in every limb and feature" (315). The killing of the sow-mother in *Lord of the Flies* provides a comparable moment (though with none of the comedy of Gulliver), for it is the unmistakably sexual element in the act, so gratuitously sadistic, that marks how fallen these boys are: boys capable of this are capable of anything (149). Jack selects with damning insight the sow-mother for slaughter, and it is the sheer wantonness of the deed, the willed excess, that relates it to gang rape, to a "wilding" in Central Park. Not just the killing itself, but the way she is killed and the orgiastic release of her killers, signal the end of innocence. These are the wanton boys of Gloucester's terrible indictment, killing for sport; even worse, they are de Sade's boys, torturing for sexual gratification.

Simon excepted, all are to some degree guilty. Piggy is never more mistaken than in his eagerness to blame the others, Jack in particular (154). Golding, following Swift, does not absolve anyone: he indicts an entire species, not some uniquely deviant members of it. Suppose that Jack had been killed in the crash and so had not vaulted, Dracula-like, onto the platform at the outset to begin his duel with Ralph; suppose that the boys had stayed good democrats, waiting in exemplary style for rescue, cooperating in the best Pelagian tradition with their own salvation. It would have ruined Golding's story, just as Hamlet's stabbing of Claudius in act 3 would have ruined Shakespeare's play. As early as chapter 4 the ship would have spotted the signal fire and rescued the boys before their descent into hell. The little boy with the birthmark would, regrettably, be dead—but as a result, at worst, of negligence, not malice. Simon and Piggy would still be alive, and the whole party, with the officer's congratulations on a jolly good show, would have been carried back to—what? Not, assuredly, safety. "The smoke of home" coming from the funnel of the departing ship after which Ralph pines (73) is a grim irony—Britain has been reduced to incinerated ash in a nuclear strike. The war will proceed apace, the dead parachutist fall from heaven to lie in undisturbed corruption on the mountaintop. The island, pigs, butterflies, and all, will return to the tranquil rhythms of its prehuman routines, but the great outside world will still require its rescue, not just because of its Jacks and Rogers, but—much more alarmingly—because of its "good" men, its Ralphs and Piggys. For, as St. Paul says, there is not one that does good (Rom. 3:10–12). That is why Ralph weeps at the close to the discomfiture of his obtuse savior—he knows, with a maturity denied to the uncomprehending adult who sees everything and understands nothing, that the longed-for "rescue" is merely a stay of execution. He weeps for the darkness of man's heart, not for the exceptional depravities of the deviant few. The home counties are in the dock with the jungle. Good boys did not become wicked in the jungle; bad boys will not be absolved by removing them to civilization.

Nowhere is Swift more relevant to *Lord of the Flies* than in the startling change of perspective that is the tale's resolution. A pack of blood-crazed hunters led by a savage autocrat suddenly dwindles into a rabble of filthy urchins headed by a little red-haired boy with broken spectacles dangling from his waist. Which of these vastly different, totally incompatible views is the truth? Even to pose the question is to expose its pointlessness: it is foolish to demand truth where there is only perspective. Remove the officer and Jack is the prince of hell, as terrifying within his domain as a Nero or a Stalin in his; restore the adult and he is a snot-nosed little brat in bad need of a wash. Context determines identity.

No other writer has so dramatically rendered the principle of perspective as Swift. Despite Dr. Johnson's notoriously unjust dismissal of Swift's achievement—a mere matter of thinking of big and little people and everything else automatically followed[26]—most readers have rightly hailed the creator of Lilliput and Brobdingnag as one of the great masters of perspective in literature. Who is Gulliver? There is, clearly, no single answer. In Brobdingnag he has the finest limbs in the world and a complexion fairer than a nobleman's three-year-old daughter. In Lilliput he is a repulsive spectacle, the stumps of his beard stronger than a boar's bristles, his complexion a mix of disagreeable colors. Which is he, beautiful or ugly? It depends entirely upon where he is and who is looking. *Esse est percipi*: the reality of things is what is assigned to them. Gulliver's gorge rises in the bedrooms of the Brobdingnagian maids of honor as he contemplates with disgust the blotches and blemishes of the "beauties" for whom every Brobdingnagian male is sighing; he is sickened by the Giant Queen's table manners, though among her own people she is considered a fastidious lady with a puny appetite (145). In the age of Bishop Berkeley as in that of Albert Einstein, truth is relative. In the "real" world beyond Lilliput and Golding's island, Gulliver will cease to be the Man Mountain and Jack, at least pro tempore, must give up being the Chief. Evaluation shifts of necessity with the shifting perspectives of the text—Jack is tyrant *and* brat—and to dismiss this virtuoso display as a gimmick is on a par with Dr. Johnson's insulting disparagement of Swift's genius.

Golding found his cue in the masterly interplay between Lilliput and Brobdingnag when he came to create his little devils, no less demonic for being childish, startlingly yet simultaneously both. There is a moment in the *Travels* that anticipates the stunning peripeteia of *Lord of the Flies*. Gulliver's fiercely patriotic account of the political struggles and continental wars of his native land provokes the Giant King to ask derisively if he is a Whig or a Tory (146). This contemptuous view of English political antagonisms—a matter of life and death to their participants but childishly insignificant to the king—has its parallel in the officer's condescending allusion to "fun and games" in *Lord of the Flies* (221). The island shrivels while Ralph, just rescued from hideous death, sobs uncontrollably, but the officer sees only playground pranks, childish cantrips.

There is, of course, one massive difference between king and officer. For Swift, the king is almost miraculously exemplary, above all in his breathtaking rejection of the offer of gunpowder—he is the answer to our problems, had we the magnanimity to follow him, a rescuer in every sense. The officer, by contrast, is all too plainly part of the problem; the nuclear warship beyond the lagoon reveals that there is no Giant King in *Lord of the Flies* to condemn the murderous ingenuity of western man—the reader must enact that role.

Hence the crucial importance of the reader at the close when he is required by the text to cooperate in making explicit what is implied. The first-person narrative of the *Travels* empowers Gulliver to express the meaning of his tale; Golding, however, must rely upon the reader to detect this for himself. It must be said that he has not always been well served in this respect. Yet the parallels between the two conclusions should make all clear. There are in both texts an expulsion—Gulliver from the tranquil society of the horses, Ralph from the frenzied tribe; an attempt by savages to kill the hero, leaving him wounded—Gulliver will carry to the grave the mark of the tribesman's arrow, Ralph's side is torn by the Chief's spear and he will suffer lifelong the psychological scars of his island experience; and, finally, a rescue that is problematic, somehow flawed and incomplete—in a sense, no rescue at all.

Gulliver is taken against his will on board Don Pedro's ship; almost immediately he tries to jump overboard, preferring to perish in the sea or risk the murderous savages rather than return to the home for which he once pined. Only when Don Pedro threatens to chain him to the bed does he reluctantly consent to be carried back to the cesspit (as he now regards Europe) from which he has escaped. What once grieved him—exile among the horses—has since become cause for ecstatic celebration. The horses' refusal to grant him asylum induces despair and Don Pedro's generous offer of free transport home—an offer that would have delighted him before his conversion—has to be forced upon him. What he has learned on the island has transformed his outlook on life. Don Pedro, in compelling him to resume the life suspended by his exile, might easily have cited Rousseau's famous paradox about forcing men to be free, had it been available in 1726. From Don Pedro's perspective, Gulliver is being made to do what he should want to do: men *must* desire rescue above all else. This, too, is the first article of Ralph's creed throughout *his* exile and it baffles him that his companions are not so fervent about it. Don't they *want* to be rescued?, he asks Piggy in anguished incredulity (153–54). Don Pedro experiences a similar bafflement as he confronts his demented castaway.

The fact that Ralph has been so uncompromising about the paramountcy of rescue—the boys should prefer to die rather than let the signal fire go out, he dramatically insists, while his auditors giggle in irresponsible embarrassment at such rhetoric (88)—makes it all the more ironic that when rescue finally comes, it should be so strangely unsatisfactory. "We'll take you off" (222)—Ralph should be overjoyed at hearing these words, the granting of his heart's desire, but plainly he is not. Certainly, he is not *averse* to rescue, as Gulliver is— Gulliver is being driven from paradise, whereas Ralph is being plucked out of hell. But this simply makes his reaction the more intriguing. To explain this is to reach to the core of the book's meaning.

To begin with, the boys have not earned rescue in the way that Ralph has continually recommended. The fire that attracts rescue is not the signal fire he so passionately campaigned for but the wicked fire of the death hunt, which leaves the island charred and uninhabitable. (What would these berserk savages have eaten had the officer not arrived to save them from the consequences of their criminal folly?) Like Iago, caring nothing for his own survival provided he can destroy Othello, Jack thinks only of killing Ralph; the prospect of a devastated island never enters his mind. Ralph is saved from destruction, Jack from self-destruction. "The fools! The fools! . . . what would they eat tomorrow?" (218–19). There is a biblical echo here: tomorrow we die. It is a remarkable exclamation: the prey troubled for the predators' survival, while they, animal-like, are obsessed solely with the appetite of the moment. There is irony, too, for it is Ralph himself who will soon be eaten—yet, caregiver and worrier throughout, he continues to care for his erstwhile companions even when he is being hunted to apparently unavoidable death.

After such knowledge, what forgiveness? As much as Gulliver, Ralph is transformed by his island experience. Gulliver's is a double vision—of Houyhnhnm perfection and Yahoo filth. Ralph's is single— an insight into the darkness of the human heart. (The degree to which Golding's vision is double is examined in the final chapter of this study.) It is, significantly, of Piggy that Ralph thinks, and that brutal death, in terms of the allegory, marks the extinction of common sense and rational thought by manic power-worship and sadism. Ralph weeps because he sees that his own personal rescue, so crucial in one respect, is, from another perspective, trivial, perhaps even deceptive.

The patronizing rescuer is merely another version of the same darkness that broke Piggy in pieces and reduced the island to mayhem.

As much as Yahoo and beau, Jack and the officer, however superficially distinct, are brothers; men like the officer may as easily destroy the planet as Jack destroys the island. That the officer would be outraged at the comparison is no proof of its inappropriateness. Once again, *Gulliver's Travels* supplies the clue. Gulliver has been taught to see the resemblance between Yahoos and men; those without the benefit of Houyhnhnm tuition are blind to the identification and resent it when made, dismissing it as the last aberration of a fool who has lost everything on the horses, the bankrupt gambler par excellence. Gulliver, for his part, sees that his rescuer is a Yahoo like himself; that Don Pedro so handsomely offers to carry Gulliver back to civilization cannot alter his perception that this civilization is the heart of Yahoodom—why should he feel grateful for such a removal? Don Pedro does not, of course, see things in this light—how could he without a sojourn in Houyhnhnmland? How can you know what you have never learned, especially when it is the scandalously subversive opposite of all you have always been taught? Don Pedro is a good European—or, in Gulliver's terms, a complacent Yahoo. For him, Gulliver must be a madman; but this is too facile a solution for the reader of the *Travels*, for he, too, has lived in Houyhnhnmland, sharing the experience, participating in the fall.

The same is true of the confrontation between Ralph and the officer at the close of *Lord of the Flies*. The boy weeps while the uneasy, embarrassed adult waits for the little scapegrace—an English boy surely ought to be able to put up a better show than this—to regain control of himself. It is the entirely predictable response of a conventional English sailor to a shameful exhibition from a countryman, however juvenile. Pity, embarrassment, shame—all compete for precedence in the adult's mind. But Ralph has lived and learned on the island, and the reader has shared this experience. The reader must side with this child who has been forced to put away childish things; it is the officer who is, paradoxically, immature, an overgrown boy, the child who takes an adult view of the human situation. The Gospel warning against the man who is a *Kinderschander*, a scandalizer of children, is stood on its head, for it is the adult who is innocent, the child who has eaten the apple.

Lord of the Flies and *Heart of Darkness* are strikingly similar in the final ironic confrontation of childlike naïveté and dark experience. If anything, Golding has the edge, since his knower is a twelve-year-old boy, while the equivalent of Conrad's ethereal dreamer, Kurtz's

Intended, is a naval officer on military service. In a striking reversal of roles, it is the officer who belongs to the nursery while it is the boy who, like Leontes, has drunk and seen the spider.[27] We are not embarrassed for Ralph; whatever disdainful pity we have to spare is for the foolish officer, not the knowing child. Ralph and reader together see that the rescue is but a temporary and unstable reprieve. He is being taken from a little hunt to a global one, for the hunters, like the Yahoos, are everywhere, and the truly fearsome killers are the nuclear warriors of civilization rather than the painted savages of nature. It is Gulliver's perception, made relevant to the even more desperate circumstances of twentieth-century history. Neither text offers escape from nature into civilization or from civilization into nature; there is no true rescue in either.

Whatever flimsy excuse can be offered for missing the implicit indictment of civilization recurring throughout the text is irrievably canceled by the unmistakable irony of the climax. Yet some readers uncomprehendingly dismiss this as a gimmick, Golding sacrificing the text's seriousness to a piece of sensationalism.[28] The truth is that the final startling change of perspective is integral to the book's meaning. It has, nevertheless, been astonishingly misinterpreted as an unprincipled evasion of the problems posed by the fable: the horror of the boys' island experience is finally only a childish, if viciously nasty, game; adult sanity has returned and the little devils will have to behave themselves again. Human nature cannot be so irremediably bad if the arrival of one adult can immediately put everything to rights—the problem is, apparently, a mere matter of classroom control.

Such obtuseness in the face of the text's irony is inexcusable. Ralph is saved, but that does not exempt us from scrutinizing his savior or assessing the fate that awaits the rescued boy. Ralph weeps for all men, the officer and his crew included. The officer's failure to see this does not entitle the reader to be equally blind. The idea that when the cruiser arrives, the beast slinks back abashed into the jungle to await the next set of castaways is so preposterous that is scarcely needs refuting.

There is no happy ending nor anything optimistic about the final scene. Whatever we may wish, it is not legitimate to infer from the text that society, the polis, is man's salvation. This book is not an implicit tribute to the humanizing power of social institutions, nor does it offer the city as a refuge from the jungle. Perhaps the city is essential, but that very much depends on what kind of city it is— Cain's city will not help us. If man regresses in nature, that does not mean that social man is necessarily good; Swift detests the Yahoo, but abhors the "civilized" Yahoos of London and Dublin even more. Of course, man needs a structured community in which to develop his humanity; of course, the city should be the safe and sheltered haven. But *should* is not *is*; in *King Lear* the castle is where man should be safe, the wild heath where he should be at risk, but Lear and Gloucester do not find it so. Golding likewise knows that all too tragically in our century the city itself has become, paradoxically, a jungle, the wild place in which man finds himself born.

   Lord of the Flies is a trap as cunningly constructed as *Gulliver's Travels*: each presents our salvation as perilously problematic and neither produces the savior we so desperately require.

5

Caliban's Freedom

The ongoing debate about Golding's literary status is radically different from the customary controversies concerning novelists' reputations. Such arguments usually have to do with the kind of novelist someone is, with the merits and the shortcomings of the craft, with technical skill or ineptitude: in a word, whether the writer in question is a good novelist or a bad one. With Golding, by contrast, the debate is conducted at a more basic level—it is a matter of his right to be called a novelist at all.

For some critics, Golding has willfully jettisoned too much of the novel's legacy, too much of what is intrinsic to the form, to qualify as inheritor and perpetuator of the great tradition. In his art of excision the surgery is too ruthlessly severe; he cuts away too many vital elements, reduces the body of the novel, so abundantly ample in the work of the great nineteenth-century realists, to something spare and sparse, almost skeletal. Where Dickens and Tolstoy seek to render the plenitude of the world, forever striving to include and extend, Golding, like Beckett, excludes and restricts, stripping the world to its bare essentials.

Where in *Lord of the Flies* is that concern with money, with the precarious dynamics of bourgeois society, the tension between prosperity and poorhouse, that has been so salient a feature of the novel from Defoe onward? Where is the concern with sex, that mandatory analysis of the relationships of men and women, of love and marriage and adultery, that the novel has so obsessively pursued from Richardson through Flaubert and Tolstoy to the present day? Where is that interest in the conquest of society, that theme of great expectations, that obsesses fictional characters from Stendhal's Julien Sorel to Fitzgerald's Gatsby? Where is that minute, detailed dissection of the social milieu, above all, the world of the city, man's home in the modern era, that fills the pages of Balzac, Dickens, and Joyce? Where—even to ask the question is a prodigy—where are the women, that indispensable half of humanity without whom there could be no life at all? (*Lord of the Flies* has fathers and sons, but no mothers or daughters. It is a striking omission—the sow-mother, so hideously slaughtered, is the sole female representative in the text. Here is the fall of man in the most literal sense of the word.) To conclude, where is the beef and ale, the humdrum minutiae of everyday life, that painstaking attention to the commonplace, identified by Trollope as the special monopolistic privilege of the novel form? How can any writer omit such indispensable elements and still be credited with the name of novelist? In a famous passage Henry James laments the artistic void into which Hawthorne was born, the dearth of social opportunities and the high civilization so abundantly available to a European writer. It was the lack of these things, James alleges, that made Hawthorne, albeit exquisitely, a provincial writer.[1] For Golding's censurers there is no such excuse: he willfully, inexcusably throws away the patrimony that Hawthorne so sadly lacked.

Golding's admirers, taking their cue from his own words, retort that precisely here, where he is so mistakenly attacked and undervalued, is his real achievement: he strips away the temporary, parochial, adventitious aspects of life to focus on what is abidingly important in the human condition, what links us with Sophocles and the Bible rather than with the paraphernalia of a particular civilization. His subject is Man, the permanent, transcendental being, rather than the merely social creatures who live their stunted lives and find their paltry definition within the unstable matrix of some evanescent system. In raising man above the social flux, Golding has made him a richer, not a poorer, being.

This immediately sets him at odds with some of the established pieties of our time. Mikhail Bakunin's words have an axiomatic force for many today: "Outside society, man would not only be unfree, but he would not even have developed into a true man."[2] The character of Simon in *Lord of the Flies* makes plain that Golding profoundly disagrees; any attempt to confine Simon within the limits of a social system is fated to fail, yet Simon is clearly intended to be the truest, the freest, human being in the book—proof that if *men* must live in society, *man*, simply to *be* man, must also live somewhere else. Detractors may say that Simon is incomprehensible; he is, most certainly, incomprehensible in purely social terms.

"What man *is*, whatever man is under the eye of heaven, that I burn to know and that—I do not say this lightly—I would endure knowing" (*Moving*, 199). The heightened, evocative language, the metaphor of heaven's eye, indicate just how profoundly elemental a cognitive ambition this is. It is a knowledge not to be garnered from government records and social statistics—one might as sensibly seek the soul with the aid of a microscope; it belongs to the poet's vocation, not the scientist's regimen. Golding seeks to unearth the human nature, constant, enduring, that underlies all the vicissitudes of history, all the manifold cultural systems within which that nature unfolds. For him, nature is the basic entity, culture the secondary development. He is, of course, not hostile to society: "Society, taken whole, is a good thing. It enables us to use our bright side. When we fall off, we fall off into our dark side" (Biles, 43–44). Nevertheless, it is the nature of man that shapes society, not vice versa (Biles, 46). Given bad people, declares Golding, no political system, however good, will work; given good people, any system will: "a good system with bad men will turn into hell . . . a bad system with good men will be a good deal nearer what you want it to be than hell is" (Biles, 50). People come first, man is ontologically prior to society. That Golding should so provocatively challenge some of the sacred shibboleths of our time underlines his commitment to the concept of a human nature underlying social forms and helps in some way to explain the startling omissions in his art.

He desiderates a kind of novel that "tries to look at life anew, in a word, for intransigence" (*Hot Gates*, 132; see also 105). *Lord of the Flies* exhibits this intransigence in its stark refusal to comply with the novel-reading expectations of the general public. The repeated tributes to Golding's originality—"the most original and imaginatively exciting" of contemporary novelists (Page, 8); someone who has "done more for the modern British novel than any of the recent novelists who have emerged" (Peter, 592)—are unquestionably linked to his decision to break with the established conventions of English fiction. If, as Sir Victor Pritchett contends, the essence of the novelist's art, especially in England, is the quotidian, one must pronounce Golding to be the most un-English of novelists.[3] (This dissident quality, as the debt to Dostoyevski makes plain, is as evident in the subject matter as in the style—both morally and artistically he stands outside the main English tradition.) "You've got to write your own books and nobody else's"

(Biles, 15). It may seem a surprising statement from someone whose first books seem to have been born of some creative quarrel with an earlier text, conceived in fertile contradiction; yet no one, friend or foe, will deny that Golding has written his own books—it is for doing so that he has been at once so highly praised and so severely censured.

In emphasizing the originality of the work, his admirers simultaneously declare the futility of judging it by irrelevant criteria imported from a more conventional fiction. They point out that "in his very first novel, he cut himself loose at a single stroke from two centuries of tradition in the English novel: centuries during which the realistic mode had been paramount," and the result has been "a different kind of narrative," a body of work that stood apart from the mass of contemporary fiction and had to be judged on its own terms (Page, 11). Golding's recoil from this traditional subject matter points to "a preoccupation with something that lies beyond that representation or imitation of individual and social realities which had been the bread and butter of novelists from Daniel Defoe to Evelyn Waugh. Golding's concern is with larger, more fundamental and abstract issues that may be called metaphysical or theological. Such works ask not 'How does man live?' but 'What manner of creature is man?'" (Page, 11). In rejecting a fiction that deals with the means of life for an older tradition of fiction that interrogates life's meaning, "Golding's achievement has been to revalidate this alternative tradition for the modern world" (Page, 11).

It is because he has forsaken the world of customary social relationships, the ordinary universe of the quotidian and circumstantial, the recognizable world that we all inhabit, that Golding seems so remote from the mainstream, so alien to the great tradition. His interests lie elsewhere. He wishes to show us what human beings are really like, not in the subaltern roles assigned them by society—wives, husbands, lovers, citizens, workers, and so on—but as souls or essences, relieved of all secondary impedimenta. We must, accordingly, discard those expectations appropriate to the realistic novel and prepare to return to an older, prenovelistic, "religious" literature, a fiction preceding humanism. Golding is closer to Bunyan than to George Eliot: *The Pilgrim's Progress* belongs to the same spiritual world as *Lord of the Flies*, *Middlemarch* to that secular world which both reject. Bunyan's book opens as *Gulliver's Travels* ends, in decisive repudiation of the social roles allotted to us; like *Lord of the Flies*, both texts tell us that if society is our only home then we are indeed lost souls, dwellers in a City of Destruction, in Yahoodom, on a demented island. George Eliot, by contrast, despite seeing much to amend in it, takes society for granted—where else can we live? Only at the close of *Daniel Deronda*, in the unsatisfactory, defective half of that novel, does she even come close to hinting that our society is no fit habitat for human beings or their true aspirations. By contrast, on the opening page of Bunyan's text, his hero turns away from home and family, from every social and civic duty, from his given roles as husband, father, and citizen, to go questing after eternal life—the life that George Eliot finds so unbelievable. Yet this incredible life, not the world of Mr. Worldly Wiseman with its sensible aims and practical priorities, not the attractions and distractions of Vanity Fair so dear to the novelist, is what matters for Bunyan's hero. It is Worldly Wiseman who points the route of the novel's progress; Bunyan has another road to follow. For Golding, as for Bunyan, those who live contentedly immersed in social categories have forfeited what is most precious to man; the social world is too much with them—their true selves lie stifled beneath an Alps of trivia.

Golding is sometimes praised in ways that plainly reveal an unease with the achievement. Angus Wilson pays tribute to him as a maker of fables rather than a novelist, revealingly hailing *Free Fall* as coming closest to "the fully felt social novel that the English have constructed in their great tradition" (Wilson, 21). One recalls F. R. Leavis's identifying *Hard Times* as the best of Dickens's books: in each case the text chosen to illustrate the achievement indicates, in fact, a certain lack of sympathy with the *oeuvre*. Kingsley Amis is franker when he criticizes the narrow and remote world of Golding (he is referring specifically to *Pincher Martin*) and begs Golding to "turn his gifts to the world where we have to live"[4]—for him, demonstrably not the world of Pincher's rock or Beelzebub's island. So often we define in advance what the novel should be, requiring it to conform to these prior expectations; when it defies these, we revenge ourselves by denying it the name of novel, calling it fable or romance instead.

Yet what Amis condemns as irrelevance, as willed and perverse oddness, a deliberate removal from reality, is seen by others as the most urgently pertinent of modern fictions. Golding is "making statements all the time about John Smith, Twentieth Century citizen. Writing about schoolboys, Neanderthalers and dead sailors appears to him to be a simple means of turning a light on contemporary human nature" (Green, 39). *Lord of the Flies* is only superficially an exotic island adventure; with the officer's arrival it becomes inescapably clear that it is our own story we have been unwittingly reading. For Amis to ask Golding to turn his gifts to the world we live in is equivalent to David, irritated and still uncomprehending, requiring Nathan to tell a more relevant tale. *Lord of the Flies* is shockingly, offensively relevant to the world we live in; its apparent abnormality of situation is merely a ruse, a strategy for obviating a too precipitate resentment, precisely the tactic of Nathan toward David. What has the story of the rich man and the robbed lamb to do with the death of Uriah and the taking of his wife? No more than the misdeeds of stranded schoolboys to the problems of modern man.

The solution to this otherwise intractable impasse between censurers and admirers, the condemners of the remoteness and the praisers of the urgency, must be sought in a more precise evaluation of the kind of statements that Golding makes. They are not, clearly, the customary secular statements that Amis demands: statements of social significance, concerning marriage, money, and careers. They are religious statements because Golding is a religious novelist, more at home with the spiritual world than with the transactions of secular society. His central concern is not the humanist one of man's relationship to man, but the larger question of man's relationship to the universe or to God. Simon, once again, is proof of this primacy: he is killed by human beings, but it is nature that conducts his obsequies. For those who insist that man is the sum of his social roles, that there can be no transcendence, Simon must be relegated to the realm of mumbo jumbo; he is certainly not to be comprehended in social terms. Golding's fiction takes us back beyond humanism, beyond our distracting modern obsession with the impedimenta of society, to the values of *Everyman* and *The Pilgrim's Progress*. Those for whom metaphysics is obscurantist nonsense will spurn such a return as misguided or even dangerous, a detour from the humanist highway of the conventional novel into some superstitious sidetrack. For such readers Golding will have small appeal. Work that "virtually excludes the normal range of human relationships which the novel covers" is ipso facto condemned; an imagination that deliberately distances itself from "the full body of human life" is perverse and irresponsible (Green, 51).

Admirers reply that too often, especially in modern fiction, the body of human life has become obese, overblown and sluggish, and that Golding should be praised for getting rid of this dropsical excess. Golding himself has been explicitly unapologetic about his alleged failure to be "engaged" or relevant. In answer to a questionnaire asking how the writer should react to the social and political questions of the day, he insists that the real task is to show man his image *sub specie aeternitatis* (in the light of eternity), not in the fleeting concerns of the moment but in what is basic in the human condition (Hynes, 3). He disdains what is local, specific, particular, and upholds what is universal, exemplary, paradigmatic. The aim is to explore what man truly *is* when all his social disguises have been taken from him. This is why Golding is the dramatist of the extreme situation, for truth lives in emergency, not in the set routines of everyday life.

"It is the extreme situation that best reveals what we are essentially . . . [t]he man in the violent situation reveals those qualities least disposable in his personality, those qualities which are all he will have to take into eternity with him."[5] Flannery O'Connor's words are sharply pertinent to *Lord of the Flies*; it is, to take one instance, only within the nightmarish extremity of the island that Roger fully acknowledges the dark truth of his inner self and gives it delicious release. The island does not make him a sadist; it simply allows him to be his true self. It is a liberation into authenticity, Caliban's freedom.

The idea that society is a clutter wherein these true, essential selves may be muffled and lost, is the key to Golding's fiction. In her essay, "The Novel Démeublé," Willa Cather contends that "the novel, for a long while, has been overfurnished," too conspicuously the domain of the property man; she attributes this state of affairs to the malign influence of Balzac.[6] His attempt to reproduce on paper the actual city of Paris—houses, upholstery, food, wines, and all—may have been a stupendous ambition, but one unworthy of an artist. The zest for material objects belongs more to the interior decorator, the window dresser, the showman; indulged by the writer, it results in a cluttered novel, more like a catalog, indiscriminate and promiscuous, than that shaped selection which is the essence of art. Knowing what to leave out is the hallmark of the artist. Cather sighs for a different kind of novel: "How wonderful it would be if we could throw all the furniture out of the window . . . and leave the room as bare as the stage of a Greek theatre, or as that house into which the glory of Pentecost descended" (Cather, 51). Only, Cather insists, when the novel sheds its "tasteless amplitude" will there be space for the spirit, room for the play of those abiding passions that survive the fads and fashions of the hour. Cather's cry against clutter, her protest against the novelist as property man and the novel as merely a vividly brilliant journalism, are relevant to an understanding of Golding's art. His novels might almost be an answer to Cather's prayer. He almost rivals Beckett in throwing out the furniture, clearing the clutter. Here is the stripped stage, the bare room, Cather longed for, and it is surely no coincidence that Golding's greatest debts are to Christianity and Greek drama, Cather's preferred exemplars of a renovated art.

Lives as well as novels can be choked with bric-a-brac and trivia, as Auden's poem "To the Unknown Citizen" so dispiritingly shows.

It presents man as an exclusively social creature, totally defined by his job, his trade-union membership, the newspapers he reads, the products he consumes. When we hear that he possesses "everything necessary to the Modern Man,/A phonograph, a radio, a car and a frigidaire,"[7] we concede the adjective but withhold the noun: he may be modern but he isn't man, merely a cog in a machine replaceable by an identical mass-produced replica the moment he ceases to function. Like the Unknown Soldier, he, too, has sacrificed everything for the state, has died without ever realizing that he has never truly lived. The poem exhibits a life full of nothing, a cluttered vacancy. Implicit is a cry for meaning, for a significance transcending social inanity: who will deliver me from the body of this death?—the cry of Bunyan's hero, three centuries on, from a vastly denser, more massively materialistic society, where man himself is just another commodity in the world emporium. We have become consumers and lost our souls.

"Had anything been wrong we should certainly have heard." The final line is ironic, exhibiting the speaker's obtuse arrogance— Bakunin's social man at his most crassly complacent, brother in blindness to the childish officer at the close of Golding's text. Everything is wrong in the poor parody of life just presented; that the speaker should be so well satisfied is confirmation of its nonsense. We recall Flaubert's merciless dissection of the squandered life in "A Simple Heart," the desolation of Bellow's Henderson contemplating in dismay the littered room of the old woman he has just roared to death: "Oh, shame, shame! Oh, crying shame. How can we? Why do we allow ourselves? What are we doing? The last little room of dirt is waiting. Without windows. So for God's sake make a move, Henderson, put forth effort. You, too, will die of this pestilence. Death will annihilate you and nothing will remain, and there will be nothing left but junk. Because nothing will have been and so nothing will be left. While something still *is*—*now*! For the sake of all, get out."[8] In a panic at meaninglessness, Henderson makes his move, a desperate foray into an Africa of the imagination, fleeing from the spiritual wasteland of modern America as Christian flees from the City of Destruction. The somber mood of Philip Larkin's speaker as he takes possession of the bleak room once lived in by the departed Mr. Bleaney, is a more disciplined, more restrainedly "English" equivalent of the same sense of alienation.[9]

In all four writers just cited—Auden, Flaubert, Bellow and Larkin—is a shared conviction that the life reviewed is no life at all, but the mere wraith of existence. I have come that you may have life and have it more abundantly: so promises Christ in John's Gospel. Auden's

Unknown Citizen, Flaubert's exploited drudge, Bellow's old junk-addict, Larkin's recluse in his "hired box," possess, by contrast, life at its most meager and attenuated—Eliot's little life with its dried tubers. Even to use the word for such pointless interruptions of darkness seems a betrayal.

Underlying this discontent is a nostalgia for a lost metaphysics, escape from the stunted life of society into a realm of significant being, where the soul rather than the social security card is our most precious possession. This is the territory of Golding's fiction; it is also the cause of much of the critical unease concerning his work. It is objected that, even if metaphysics were a legitimate intellectual activity, the novel is the least appropriate instrument for such complex speculation. Lurking here is the old assumption that the novel should stick to quotidian reality, eschewing these high-flown concerns, and it may be sufficient to retort that we ought not to set limits in advance on a writer of Golding's originality, since he is engaged, among other things, in redefining the nature and scope of fiction. But we have in any case the supreme example of Dostoyevski, for many the greatest of novelists, to give the lie to the objection that the novel is incapable of dealing with metaphysics. When Ivan, inviting his brother Alyosha to a chat, says, "We have first of all to solve the eternal questions" (*Karamazov*, 272), he is not, as the ensuing discussion so plainly reveals, referring to sex, social advancement, or the making or losing of money; the brothers debate the nature of evil, sadism, the existence of God, the nexus between morality and immortality, the problem of human freedom, the state as anti-Christ. Yet who will deny that *The Brothers Karamazov* is among the greatest novels ever written? What could be more "metaphysical" than a novel in which a leading character talks with the devil?

When Virginia Woolf says of the great nineteenth-century Russians that "to write of any fiction save theirs is a waste of time,"[10] the implication is that here is an excavational depth, a penetration to the roots of being, not merely unequaled but unattempted in other fiction. Of Dostoyevski it has been said that "deep down in his philosophy lay the conviction that that which is ordinary is in some sense unreal,"[11] and the exaggeration is pardonable in calling attention to his prophetic art. In order to unveil the secret of man, Dostoyevski studies him in situations of crisis rather than in his stable surroundings, the normal and rational forms of his everyday existence. Dostoyevski and Golding alike prefer the unpublished forms of being in the belief that the essential self cannot find expression in dull routine, only in some flare-up in which the fixed and dead forms of an effete society are destroyed or superseded. For both truth is chthonic, incompatible with the banality of surfaces.

In both cases, too, there is a conversion to a darker view of life, the abandonment of an earlier idealism—in Dostoyevski's case, naive Schillerism; in Golding's, a scientific humanism that had promised to make the world pellucid and man perfect. For each, conversion followed the shock of a personal experience—for Dostoyevski, the Petrashevsky affair; for Golding, World War II. Dostoyevski's resolve "to find the man in man" (*Karamazov*, xxii) entailed restoring the spiritual depths currently denied him: released from his material and social prison, man was to be a spiritual creature once more, and this Dostoyevski claimed as the highest realism, the very realism of life itself. Humanism was the real superstition, its powerlessness proven before the tragedy of human destiny. To expose this frailty Dostoyevski subjects his characters to a series of experiments, putting them into unusual situations while depriving them of the external stays of the customary social framework. In doing so, he becomes an archaeologist of human nature—going deep to lay bare its lowest, most hidden, hence truest foundations. Such archaeology entails criminology: Dostoyevski discovers that man is at heart a lawbreaker, but that, paradoxically, he breaks laws because he can find no real reason to obey them. What reader can fail to detect the anguish underlying Svidrigaylov's flippant question to Raskolnikov: "Now tell me, why on earth should I restrain myself?"[12]

The hidden pathos in Dostoyevski is a pathos of freedom—all of his novels are experiments of human liberty. Freedom is Janus-faced, at once gift and trial. Dostoyevski liberates man from all law, cosmic order included, so that he may trace his destiny in freedom. What monstrosities and perversions will follow such emancipation? Yet only in such enormities are the depths of human nature revealed, those depths which in everyday existence lie dormant and undisturbed. Are there any moral limits or is everything permitted? This is the agonizing question with which Dostoyevski's characters forever wrestle. In no other writer are the paradoxes of unlimited freedom so pertinaciously pursued. Freedom, taken to an extreme, results in murder, parricide, even servitude. In tracing these fearful consequences, Dostoyevski challenges the straightforward rationalism of earlier thinkers such as Hobbes and Mill. There can, he insists, be a will against reason, a choice of unreason for its own sake. Ralph and Piggy in *Lord of the Flies* believe naively that reason is an obligation: we *must* be reasonable once we recognize what reason is. Jack baffles and frightens them precisely because he *wants* unreason. For Dostoyevski the choice is not merely possible—it is to be expected. The same holds true for those who regard freedom as a compulsion, who deny that men can knowingly choose slavery. In "The Legend of the Grand Inquisitor" we see men doing precisely this, and on the island Golding's schoolboys make the same choice. When, at the book's close, Ralph, answering the officer's question, declares himself to be the leader, it is both untrue and undemocratic, since the boys have all too plainly, if deplorably, preferred Jack. Ralph's earlier chagrin and puzzlement stem from the fact that the boys consider Jack to be a good chief—they are willing to slaughter Ralph to prove this. All legitimate government, insist the democrats, must be based on consent; but what if men consent to servitude, what if—startling oxymoron—they are willing captives? The Grand Inquisitor and Jack rule by consent; in Dostoyevski and Golding we are shown the obsequious raptures of slaves before the might that has overawed them.

To link Golding with Dostoyevski, as with Swift, is to enhance, not diminish, his work. Stationing him in such company is a compliment; the real disparagement is to bind *Lord of the Flies* too exclusively to a minor work like *The Coral Island*, however significant as instigator, while missing the affinities with the masterpieces, *Gulliver's Travels* and *The Brothers Karamazov*. George Steiner has illuminatingly argued that the best readings of a work of art are to be found in a responding work of art, that the judgments coming from within art possess a penetrative authority rarely equalled by those propounded from without by academic critics.[13] Only in art do we find a mastery of answering form comparable to its object: Virgil "reads" Homer better than any critic; Dante renders the same service to Virgil; Milton enters into creative dialogue with all three. But there must be a commensurability between the interacting texts: *Tom Jones* congratulates Richardson by challenging him; James's *The Portrait of a Lady* honors *Middlemarch* by engaging the earlier work.

It is patently absurd to think of Golding engaging Ballantyne in such a way; there is no real commensurability or equality of import between *Lord of the Flies* and *The Coral Island*—the relationship, in one sense so overt, is, in a far more vital sense, altogether less serious, more casually adventitious. It is not just a question of Golding's being the greater work; *Anna Karenina* is a greater work than *Madame Bovary*, but it is not absurd to link them together or to note the smaller world of the one in the light of the other's transcendence. But only in the relatively unimportant matter of their external machinery of plot do *Lord of the Flies* and *The Coral Island* relate to each other.

Ballantyne is a mere occasion, a spark to ignite Golding's imagination as he composes his own radically different version of reality. To believe that a century after Ballantyne's book Golding is chiefly concerned to discredit its juvenile thesis, stretches credulity to the breaking point. There is a much more significant quarry to be hunted down—far more is at stake than the tardy rebuttal of a boys' adventure yarn by a minor nineteenth-century romancer. Far from obliterating Ballantyne, Golding has made him known to many who would otherwise never have heard of him; Golding is his publicist rather than his destroyer.

Golding needs a heresy to attack before his own imagination can take fire. The heresy targeted in *Lord of the Flies* is humanism, especially in its central doctrine of human self-sufficiency, of man not merely as the measure but the master of things:

> Glory to Man in the highest!
> for Man is the master of things.[14]

Ballantyne is merely the heresy at its weakest and most vulnerable. "If 'humanism' means a doctrine implying either that there are no limits whatever to human self-perfectibility or that people are entirely free in stating the criteria of good and evil, Christianity is certainly opposed to humanism."[15] It would be irrelevant for some modern apologist of Ballantyne to argue that he held no such views, for that, even if true, has no bearing on *Lord of the Flies*. It is humanist arrogance that Golding sets out to expose in his book; that he does so at second remove, using Ballantyne as a stalking-horse for much bigger game, need not surprise us in view of the precedent set by Dostoyevski in *The Brothers Karamazov*. The enemy nominally attacked in "The Legend of the Grand Inquisitor," the Caesaro-Papism of Roman Catholicism, is in fact a surrogate for an onslaught by Dostoyevski upon a far more dangerous, contemporary foe. The real threat is the socialism that will tyrannize the future, not the Catholicism that once tyrannized the past; it is the new inquisition that Dostoyevski fears, the repressive regime that will appear in the pages of Kafka, Koestler, and Orwell, not the one that burned Jews and heretics in sixteenth-century Spain. That ultramontanes and socialists detest each other does not prevent Dostoyevski from burying his attack upon the latter in a denunciation of the former.

Even the shade of Ballantyne protesting from the grave that he bore no responsibility for the horrors of the twentieth century would leave the impact of *Lord of the Flies* undiminished; Golding's text deals with man's predicament in the modern age; it is not, despite

surface resemblance, a simple inversion of a nineteenth-century boys'
book. Golding follows Dostoyevski in concealing the true object of his
attack; in identifying this target we shall simultaneously see the extent
to which he is Dostoyevski's heir.

Leszek Kolakowski observes, "Recent history seems . . . to suggest
that attempts, in traditionally Christian societies, to achieve a perfect
'liberation' from what radical humanists believed was man's bondage
under God's imaginary tyranny, were to threaten mankind with a more
sinister slavery than Christianity had ever encouraged" (201). The
relevance of this belief to Dostoyevski is unmistakable: he is the
prophet of this appalling apocalypse, as understandable in psychological as in theological terms. No other writer has so devastatingly attacked the heresy of self-sufficiency or so powerfully demonstrated the
disastrous consequences flowing from this arrogance. His chief theme
is the enslavement that comes from a false sense of freedom.

"Here at least / We shall be free" declares Satan as he takes his
first look at hell, and Golding's Jack—with much of Lucifer's sense of
injured merit—reaches a like conclusion: "Better to reign in Hell than
serve in Heaven."[16] "Freedom, high-day! High-day, freedom!" Caliban exults at the possibility of evading Prospero's discipline.[17] *Lord
of the Flies* is a critique of this irresponsible freedom, confirmation of
Burke's salutary monition: "The effect of liberty to individuals is, that
they may do what they please: We ought to see what it will please
them to do, before we risque congratulations, which may be soon
turned into complaints."[18] The warning modulates into outright condemnation: "But what is liberty without wisdom, and without virtue?
It is the greatest of all possible evils; for it is folly, vice, and madness,
without tuition or restraint" (373). This might easily be applied to the
behavior of Raskolnikov in *Crime and Punishment*, of Smerdyakov
instructed by Ivan in *The Brothers Karamazov*, of the knot of possessed
conspirators in *The Devils*, and of Golding's demented children on
the island. Golding's preoccupation with Ivan Karamazov's "eternal
questions"—the nature of evil, the relationship between totalitarianism and devil-worship, the fearful abysses of the unrestrained will—
has its brilliant ancestry in the novels of Dostoyevski. His themes are
those of the great Russian transposed to our own times, with one
striking difference: Golding writes after the fall, after the ghastly veri-
fications of Dostoyevski's prophetic art; what Dostoyevski dreamed is
now fact—in the twentieth century everything *is* permitted. In his
critique of arrogant humanism and untrammeled freedom, the two
major themes of *Lord of the Flies*, Golding stands revealed as Dostoyevski's inheritor. This relationship is the burden of the following pages.

Caliban's Freedom

The opening image of a schoolboy clambering through the creepers of a tropical jungle signals a striking discordance between environment and person. Lagoon, jungle, the strange bird with its witchlike cry, consort oddly with the boy dressed for some faraway classroom. The dualism of jungle and home counties is immediately visible, and "the long scar smashed into the jungle" (7), the tree trunks shredded by the crash, indicate that the relationship is adversarial and wounding—the machine in the garden in an especially violent way.

Far from being dismayed, the boy is elated at the prospect of adventure. After pulling up his stockings, in routine deference to established convention, he discards his sweater in the bath of heat and the process of divesting the things of civilization is innocuously begun. Within minutes of meeting Piggy, Ralph is entertaining the ecstatic speculation that there are no adults on the island, that children alone have survived the crash. It seems like the answer to a prayer. Adults mean rules, restrictions, obedience; without them the boys will bask in a fairy-tale freedom. Golding's is, however, a wicked fairy tale in which, as with Midas, Macbeth, and Gatsby, it is in the granting of desire, the ambush of a specious prayer, that disaster lurks. The witchlike bird recalls the opening of *Macbeth*, another story about the fall of man, of dreams delivered and ambitions accomplished, only to turn into calamities and condemnations. Macbeth's longing for kingship has its analogue in Ralph's joy at an adult-free island: "the delight of a realized ambition . . . the imagined but never fully realized place leaping into real life" (8, 16). His rapture is such that he has to force himself to accept the solidity of his surroundings—they seem too good to be true, too delectable to last.

It is as though Golding, like some sardonic god of old, decided to grant the so fatally misconceived heart's desire. Like Midas with his golden touch, Ralph will later pray for the once-craved freedom to be canceled; like Macbeth, he will come to see what he desired as a torment; and in both cases, Beelzebub, the common enemy of mankind, is crucially involved. The longed-for liberation becomes possession, the idyll a nightmare. Golding, the former student of science, sets up his laboratory experiment: you say that the unconfined freedom of an island without adults would be paradisiacal; very well, here is your paradise—let's see what you make of it.

Lord of the Flies is essentially a critique of freedom and, inseparable from this, of the humanist arrogance inculcated by a bad education. In Diderot's *Rameau's Nephew* the nephew speculates as to the outcome of letting a child grow up without any attempt to discipline him through education. Diderot, the *moi* of the dialogue, answers that such a brute, his infantile mind served by an adult body, would wring his father's neck and sleep with his mother. The nephew, unperturbed, counters: "That proves the necessity of a good education, and who is denying it?"[19]

As a schoolmaster of many years, Golding has a professional interest in education. The children in *Lord of the Flies* have been educated; but that, as events make plain, is the problem, especially if we agree with the nephew that education should be a shield against nature. Golding arranges a situation where the only discipline must come from within. Back in England, Jack and Roger would be troublesome brats, problem children, self-willed and perverse, but, finally, controllable—even if such control took the extreme form of the juvenile court; they would not be a menace. Misconduct would reap its appropriate chastisement by parents, teachers, and police. Oedipus aged three can do no harm; aged thirty, he is a monster. The jungle permits the children to become little monsters, liberating them to enact those fantasies which the adult world inhibits. On the island Jack and Roger are Hitler and Torquemada. But *Lord of the Flies* is a two-way street, its reciprocity unmistakable: if Jack and Roger are adults writ small, the adult world, so foolishly revered by Piggy, is Jack and Roger writ large. Golding has devised an exercise in proportion and its tragedy is that God, the determining factor, is missing.

"The best education of all" Alyosha tells the children in *The Brothers Karamazov*, is "some beautiful, sacred memory preserved since childhood" (911). If so, Golding's children are badly educated: an address and a telephone number scarcely qualify as sacred or beautiful. These children are, in fact, the victims of a ruinous education. "Here was a coral island" (15): Ballantyne is the immediate culprit as purveyor of the fallacious mythology associated with this expression. The idea of fiction in Plato's sense of harmful lies has been a major theme in the novel from Cervantes onward. The damage that books do: this is the burden of *Don Quixote, Northanger Abbey, Eugene Onegin, Madame Bovary*. In our own time the accusation has been extended to films, as in Nathanael West's *Day of the Locust*. The dissemination of disinformation, the inculcation of false views of reality, through a lying art, has worried moralists from Plato to our own day. No girl was ever seduced by a book, according to the wisecrack of Jimmy Walker, onetime mayor of New York. Dante disagrees. Among those being punished in hell for sins of the flesh he meets Francesca da Rimini and hears her blame a lubricious book for her adultery with her brother-in-law:

The book was Galleot, Galleot the
complying
Ribald who wrote; we read no more
that day.[20]

Reading can seriously damage your spiritual health.

But literature can have its wider seductions, not simply as pornography but as false teaching, a screen before reality. To trust a false book is as dangerous as living in a condemned building or putting to sea in a leaky boat: reality will have its revenge. Yet fictions, as Plato's opponents from Aristotle onward insist, can save as well as ruin. *Lord of the Flies* is intended to be a saving fiction. Golding arraigns *The Coral Island*, even though Ballantyne is merely the pretext for a larger indictment. The boys are at risk because they mistake Ballantyne's dream for reality, as astray as Quixote with his tomes of chivalry or Emma Bovary with her tales of romance.

"It's like in a book" (38). *The Coral Island* is the wrong book, an education for disaster, a preparation for hell—as much as Francesca, the boys might blame literature for their fall. The dangers of a bad education are manifest from the outset. Ralph is already dreaming of coral islands while Piggy, the adult disguised as a child—his premature baldness is already detectable—sensibly but impotently warns him of their predicament. Despite his poor eyesight, Piggy has seen that the pilot is dead and will not, as Ralph so airily assumes, be returning to them. There will be no instant rescue; the children are abandoned. But, for the enraptured Ralph, abandonment holds no terrors.

Jack is just as confident. The realization that they are alone, without an adult to guide or supervise, stimulates him to an impressive show of self-reliance. "Then we'll have to look after ourselves" is his admirably decisive rejoinder to the news, words reiterated by Ralph at the first assembly (22). But it is mere show, braggadocio posturing: behind the brave words is a childish helplessness—looking after themselves is what the boys so signally fail to do. Deprived of adult authority, they cannot survive. Within the allegory this can only be interpreted as a questioning of humanism, of that axiomatic self-sufficiency exhorted and expected by Feuerbach and George Eliot. The thrust of their teaching is that since God has been shown to be merely the projection of man, so man must resume the functions once erroneously assigned to the figment: man will become his own redeemer, will have to look after himself—what has to be done will be done. The argument is carried to its extreme with the more bellicose Bakunin: God's death is celebrated as an indispensable stage in man's maturation—God must die so that man may cease to be a child. Here, rather than in the rebuttal of Ballantyne, is the momentous debate at the heart of *Lord of the Flies*.

Jack's arrogance should alert us to the fact that more is involved than the demolition of Ballantyne's blunders. Jack exhibits at once the imperialist mentality of human beings toward the external world and its especially offensive variant in the chauvinism that Golding attributes to his countrymen. "We've got to have rules and obey them. After all, we're not savages. We're English; and the English are best at everything" (47). Jack, it might be argued, was not born thinking himself superior—his is a cultural rather than a genetic arrogance. The truth is that he displays human insolence carried to its outrageous extreme in the person of its English exponents, something we have already remarked in the unenlightened Gulliver newly arrived in Houyhnhnmland.

It is a fitting judgment on Jack's complacency that he should be metamorphosed into the Chief, fiercest savage of them all, brutally rejecting the rules in favor of naked power: "Bollocks to the rules! We're strong—we hunt!" (100). Yet the island is for Jack an education in the etymological sense: it brings him out, supplying the opportunity to be what he truly is, not changing but freeing him. Who or what is responsible for Jack? In *The Brothers Karamazov* Ivan learns in horror that he has taught Smerdyakov to be a parricide—Ivan longs for Dmitry's guilt, for that would confirm Ivan's innocence. But Smerdyakov, the vulgarization of Ivan, in claiming the murder for his own, simultaneously claims Ivan as begetter and accomplice. In a vain attempt to repudiate responsibility for Smerdyakov, Ivan goes mad.

Who taught Jack to be the insufferable jingoist he is? If the idiom of his remark is childish, the sentiment is straight from the adult world. The easy answer is to blame Ballantyne, but behind Ballantyne, as behind Smerdyakov, stands another, more important criminal. As Smerdyakov is the vulgarization of Ivan, so Ballantyne is the vulgarization of Feuerbach: these are the ideological instigators, the primal culprits. In *Lord of the Flies* it is the arrogance of man that is in the dock, not simply its English subset, however offensive that may be. Fault has been found with the latest film version of Golding's book for changing the children from English schoolboys to American cadets—thereby, it is alleged, spoiling the whole point of the book. Without justifying the change, the objection seems spurious. *Lord of the Flies* deals with the fall of man, not the pharisaism of one particular nation, and Americans are, presumably, as fallen as anyone else. Lionel Trilling remarked that American boys would not so completely have forgotten homes and families as these English youngsters apparently do, but, true or not, it would be wrong to infer from this that Golding is simply attacking the English (quoted in Johnston, 10). English arrogance is savaged in *Lord of the Flies*, not because the English have a monopoly, but because they exhibit the failing at its most flagrant. Nevertheless, as with Swift, the target is man in general, not simply the defective products of the English educational system.

Golding accuses the English because he believes, to his credit, that criticism begins at home. In addition, his countrymen, with their curious idea of themselves as a kind of immaculate conception, stand in particular need of correction, not because they are worse but because they deludedly imagine themselves better. Orwell was similarly motivated in deciding to make London the capital of his nightmare regime: it can happen to the English as easily as to anyone else, and the risk is the greater the more people believe themselves exempt from the threat.

That the boys' experience is intended to be universally applicable is evident from the image of the boat-shaped island, home of the human voyage, and the categorical proprietary claim of the boys surveying it: "This belongs to us" (31). Man's dominion over nature is axiomatic to Western thinking. "This is our island," proclaim the boys in a proprietary ecstasy that brooks no demur; pigs and butterflies, chronological precedence notwithstanding, do not count, for we are the inheritors (38). Not only that—we are also the best custodians; the world is ours and is safe in our charge. The conviction has its roots in Judeo-Christian beliefs about creation, but it survived the discrediting of Genesis to remain the cornerstone of a secular civilization. Precisely here is the problem. What has been forgotten is that in the myth man is God's steward, and, as Fall and Flood make so depressingly clear, there is no guarantee that he will govern wisely and well. The promise is conditional: if man remembers his ultimately subordinate status, he will be a good gardener; this is our island—under God. When man rejected God and became a law unto himself, the idea of holding the world in trust, of a final accounting when he would be asked to justify his stewardship, was lost: this is our island to do with as we please. Can it be denied that some such attitude has determined man's relationship to the world, at least since the Enlightenment? Can it equally be denied that its practical consequences, great advances notwithstanding, have been ruinous and potentially catastrophic? If the garden is ever reduced to a cesspit or to radioactive ash, it will not be pigs and butterflies but men who are responsible. At the core of Golding's parable is a demand for accountability. That Golding back in 1954 may not have intended any such ecological warning need not deter us from remarking it, since he himself has sensibly resigned any sort of "patria potestas over his brain-children," thus inviting critics legitimately to discover what the author himself has never considered (*Hot Gates*, 100).

There is from the outset something ominous in the boys'attitude to their new surroundings: "They savoured the right of domination. . . . They were lifted up" (32). It is the kind of mind-set that in Judeo-Christian and Greek tradition alike carried the promise of retribution, the chastisement of the pride that goes before a fall, of the superbia, the excessive self-esteem, that demands nemesis. Only a sense of reverence toward the world so cavalierly appropriated could palliate the presumption, but this is what is so criminally lacking. "This belongs to us" (31). No one can challenge man's management of creation, for his is finally the unanswerable defiance of Goneril: "Who can arraign me for it?"[21] Golding compels us to reexamine our ideas about our position in the universe—or whether, in medieval man's sense, we have any position at all. "We're explorers" (27): it is Ralph, spokesman for decency and fair play, who says this, and in our own day we have seen all too deplorably the consequences of man's exploration of nature: depletion of the ozone layer, deforestation, pollution, all the sad characteristics of the global order that has come to dominate the world. Austerity and humility are as conspicuously absent from this order as they are from the boys' administration of the island.

Do we own ourselves, let alone the world? Jack in the grip of his murderous compulsion, Roger uncontrollably lusting to inflict pain upon another human being, the boys in a state of frenzied possession: these are scarcely an argument for the ability of human beings to take care of themselves. Their right to rule the garden and to control the other animals is equally problematic. Golding's assertion that the animals do not belong to us throws a searchlight on the boys' behavior on the island (*Hot Gates*, 103). More, obviously, is involved in the killing of pigs than the simple procurement of meat. Jack is as avid to kill as Raskolnikov, as adept at rationalizing his compulsion. Raskolnikov offers two totally incompatible motives for slaying the old pawnbroker: first, the utilitarian, "moral" justification of the greater good; second, the "Napoleonic," immoral argument of the superman's right to defy the law. In the end, as much to himself as to anyone else, he admits the truth: he simply wants to kill; desire has become obsession. Jack, lovingly tracking the pig's droppings, is equally entranced: his argument that they need meat is a flimsy pretext for the truth that he needs blood. He enters the story as Dracula, vaulting onto the platform with flying cloak, peering into the darkness, tall, thin, and bony—repulsive and ominous from the outset. The blood that is Dracula's diet recurs as image throughout the text, usually in association with Jack, and it is totally fitting that Roger should by the close have promoted himself as chief impaler. The first pig escapes slaughter only because Jack is still conditioned by the taboos of a ruined civilization; ashamed, he fiercely seeks excuse for his "failure" to take life. But that he is not the sole culprit is revealed as the decent Ralph adopts the ferocious idiom of imperialist predators, his sahib ancestors: "You should stick a pig. . . . They always talk about sticking a pig" (33). Ralph's reading has taught him that pigs must be killed to a prescribed ritual. The boys carry this to an abominably foul extreme in the slaughter of the sow-mother, and again there is precedent in Dostoyevski's sickening description of a horse being flogged to death: "But it's only a horse and God has given us horses to be flogged" (*Karamazov*, 282).

Golding strives throughout to expose the unsound education that leaves the boys helpless before their island experience; in words and deeds alike its badness is shown. "We want to have fun. And we want to be rescued" (41): a good education would have substituted *but* for *and*. The conjunction so culpably used indicates a complacent assumption that survival will be child's play until the guaranteed rescue—they confront the island with the nonchalance of boys assured of a dinner. That life may be a matter of harsh choices, of priorities and sacrifices, never occurs to them: "We want to be rescued; and of course we shall be rescued" (41). Such crass presumption is crying out to be punished.

Behind the national trait of self-congratulation is a positivist arrogance not confined to the English: "We know what goes on and if there's something wrong, there's someone to put it right" (91). It is the religious idea of providence unjustifiably retained by a secular society, and the childishness of expression should not divert us from this fact. "You have doctors for everything . . . Life is scientific" (91–92): every disease must have a cure, every problem a solution. Implicit here is the facile antitragic temper that prompted Golding's own career switch from science to art. Life, like a five-star hotel, will infallibly supply our desires. Ralph's absurd account of the queen's room with maps of all the islands in the world—his father has told him this (41)—is precisely the kind of reassuring nonsense that the applauding boys wish to hear. There are no unknown islands left, no terra incognita (including man himself), no darkness: what is not already in the light will soon be there. There are no ghosts because the world must make sense, must be a rational and intelligible entity. "If there were a beast I'd have seen it" (91). It depends where you look. Simon will tell you: do not search the forest, search the soul. The vulgar reductionism of thinking that the beast is a material creature, something you can hunt and kill, is precisely what the Lord of the Flies derides in the interview with Simon. No more than Marlowe's Mephistophilis is Golding's devil a scientific materialist; Faustus vulgarly thinks of hell as a place of forks and brimstone, but Mephistophilis corrects him: "Why, this is hell, nor am I out of it."[22]

The boys' misjudgments would be less offensive if they were not so magisterially made. Jack's pretensions to adult competence are shown in his rejection of Christian names—kids' names, as he contemptuously calls them—and his demand to be known by his surname alone. Ralph, taken in by this pose of maturity, turns to Jack as to authority: "This was the voice of one who knew his own mind" (22). It is a ludicrously inaccurate assesment. Jack is the biggest child of them all, the spoiled child par excellence—a crybaby when thwarted, flying into tantrums when he cannot have his own way, demanding to be made chief because he can sing high C (23). It would be funny if it were not frightening. Jack is no fool, but he *is* unstable and dangerous, and the mind he knows and which Ralph so mistakenly admires, is a bad mind, violent and, above all, immature.

"This is our island. It's a good island. Until the grown-ups come to fetch us we'll have fun" (38). The hollowness of the boast is revealed when the dead parachutist lands on the mountaintop and this part of the island, so crucial to their hopes of rescue, becomes a no-go area. Only Simon has the courage to climb the peak and face the beast. Jack and his tribe retreat to an evil fortress, while Piggy is applauded by those who stay loyal to Ralph for his "brilliant" improvisation of moving the signal fire to the beach. The mountaintop, where the fire should be, is strictly off-limits—a prohibition scarcely necessary to promulgate since none of the boys, Simon aside, would dare to go there. Simon's proposal to climb the mountain provides, were confirmation required, clinching proof of his dottiness. For the boys, so abjectly to surrender the most important part of the island makes nonsense of their territorial claims: the island is manifestly *not* theirs—it, and they with it, belong to Beelzebub.

Their proposed program of fun until rescue is equally exploded, a proof of their glib self-ignorance, their childish alienation from reality. But Golding's prime aim is to show that the children do not have a corner on childishness. If the coral island mentality represents folly, the rescuing officer has sailed straight from its pages. His inane remarks not only link his childishness to theirs, but also suggest that he is still in the same parlous condition from which he has just rescued them. "I should have thought that a pack of British boys," he says, "would have been able to put up a better show than that" (222). In form and content alike this remark is puerile. The very fact that his rebuke echoes Jack's jingoist folly is enough to condemn him: how, having read the book, can we take seriously anyone who says this? When he nods "helpfully," the reader waits to see a specimen of the help he has to offer and is not surprised to hear him alluding to the coral island, repeating Ralph's original folly as he has repeated Jack's (222–23). Beside such childishness, the children seem mature; yet he is the savior. Mere size makes him the savior in their little world, but in the larger world he is simply another foolish, wicked child, with no prospect whatsoever of being saved in turn.

In Golding's exercise in proportion, the adult is to the child as God is to man. "Are there any adults—any grown-ups with you?" (221). An affirmative answer would have ruined Golding's story, for in that case there would have been no slide into savagery, no slaughter of Simon or murder of Piggy, no hunt for Ralph, no devastated island. The boys would have been rescued in chapter 4, because the signal fire would not have been allowed to go out. The proof that one able-bodied adult would have saved the children is that one does; the officer only has to step ashore and mayhem ceases—the manic savages dwindle instantly into a circle of unkempt urchins indulging in "fun and games."

There is an analogous question of equal import in *Nineteen Eighty-four* when O'Brien asks Winston if he believes in God and receives the expected negative reply. Big Brother versus Winston is the most ludicrous of mismatches; Big Brother versus God would be an altogether different matter. But there is no God in *Nineteen Eighty-four*, and, dead parachutist apart, there is no adult in *Lord of the Flies* until the closing pages. Those readers who take the ending as a straightforward rescue are interpreting the book as a simple boys' story; only those who proceed to the second level of explication avoid this error. At this level the savior requires salvation; adults are wicked, overgrown children, their potential for evil fearfully enlarged—the monsters of *Rameau's Nephew*, with infantile minds and powerful bodies.

God is the missing factor in the equation, and this absence makes the book's logic one of despair. If no adult means no rescue for the children, then no God must mean no rescue for mankind. *Lord of the Flies* provokes resistance because its message is so scandalously plain.

"At home there was always a grown-up" (102). Ralph, pining for lost authority, has come a long way from his initial ecstatic celebration of freedom. Yet it is finally the longed-for adult world that Golding accuses. Superficially a story about the disasters that befall children when adults are absent, *Lord of the Flies* is really about what happens to adults when God is dead. The outrage of its conclusion has already been adumbrated by Shakespeare and Dostoyevski:

> If that the heavens do not their visible spirits
> Send quickly down to tame these vile offences,
> It will come—
> Humanity must perforce prey on itself,
> Like monsters of the deep.[23]

For Albany, cannibalism will be the consequence of atheism. Ivan Karamazov lives to see the prophecy fulfilled: "One reptile will devour another reptile, and serve them both right" (*Karamazov*, 164). And why not, if everything is permitted?

We see here why *Lord of the Flies* is so strikingly opposed to the conventional wisdom of the English moral tradition with its assumption that religion and morality are entirely disconnected. For such a view the existence of God is a side issue, an irrelevance, with no significance for human conduct: men without God will be little different from men with him. Pascal, by contrast—and in this he is founder of a radically different tradition that includes Nietzsche, Dostoyevski and Sartre—is shocked by such criminal frivolity: for him there is no more crucially *human* question than that of God's existence; how we answer it makes all the difference to the way we live.[24]

George Eliot may stand as typical of the English moral tradition. God is a fiction, immortality a dream, but the moral law stands immovable as ever—the ten commandments survive, unshaken, the exploded myth of their discredited provenance. Nietzsche, by contrast, talks of a revaluation of *all* values—what man once chiseled in stone he may break to pieces, for these are *our* commandments, self-conferred and revocable at our discretion. Dostoyevski similarly insists that if there is no God, everything is permitted—you need only deceive the police, or, better still, command them, as Shakespeare's Goneril so starkly discloses. Sartre, too, believes that abandonment and its accompanying anguish arise from a godless universe that has no moral norms other than those we invent. It is surely obvious which of these moral systems *Lord of the Flies* belongs to; Golding is thoroughly un-English, recreant to the native pragmatic tradition, in his challenge to its complacent atheism. He has the courage of his pessimism—though we must always bear in mind that pessimism in this case is just one of morality's strategies and that *Lord of the Flies* is a highly moral book. He dares to ask man, after the atrocities of our time, if he is still so cheerfully confident of his ability to go it alone, to survive and prosper by his own unaided efforts. For the English tradition, such a question is almost indecent, not to be thought, far less articulated; one suspects that part of the adverse reaction to *Lord of the Flies* in its own country is attributable to the angry embarrassment of people watching a member of the family, who ought to know better, making a fool of himself.

Golding disdains his native tradition to follow Dostoyevski, exploring the abysses of freedom and tracking the intricate perversions to which its unfettered pursuit can lead. The completely lawless man, sunk in a horrible bog of his own free will (*Karamazov*, 430)—who but Dostoyevski would risk so audacious an oxymoron?—is the terror of his pages. Golding's Roger is a notable addition to the genus. Both writers expose the futility of a moral order relying solely on the fear of punishment. Certainly, the law must punish transgressors, but the true deterrent and final accuser should be the sense of sin within the wrongdoer; the external law which strikes the culprit is only a symbol of his inner destiny. We punish ourselves before the state does—what else is Raskolnikov's story about? The state is merely the lesser and subaltern chastiser, the reinforcer of a transcendent morality that no more depends for its operation upon earthly authority than does the weather. Murder is wrong; the Russian state simply recognizes this moral absolute—it does not validate, far less create it. Where there is no sense of sin, but merely fear of the police, moral chaos attends. Nothing is then required but to know how to act with impunity, and the terrifying result is the monsters: Smerdyakov, Svidrigaylov, Verkhovensky. For Roger in *Lord of the Flies* law is, likewise, purely external; punishment comes from without, or not at all. Where there is no possibility of external punishment—no parents, teachers or police, no coercive or retributive power—Roger is totally free to act as he will; there is nothing within to restrain or accuse him. All that stops him from stoning the littlun is conditioning—in England he would be punished, and he refrains not because it is wrong but because it is risky. Remove the risk and Roger will become the most zealous of stoners.

"When we get rid of our habits, we shall become gods" (*Karamazov*, 768). For Roger, morality is a habit that the island helps him to break. Civilization is merely a custom, a lethargy, a conditioned reflex. Jack, longing to kill the piglet, yet unable to do so, is simply unlearning a tedious, half-taught lesson; soon he will overcome the rote indoctrination as he sniffs the ground and lovingly scans the pig droppings, lusting to kill, more avid for blood than meat. The island, like a truth serum, reveals the reality beneath social routine, and its prime lesson is to confirm Renan's bleak belief that we are living on the perfume of an empty vase. Roger is simply the most extreme instance of the emptiness of civilization: to say that he retreats from it misleadingly implies that he was ever there. The island sets people free to be their true selves. Roger would have the same sadistic drives at home, but the island is an invitation to indulge them with impunity, as he finds himself in the serendipitous position of a psychopath promoted to chief of police. It is, however, not only in the jungle that psychopaths become chiefs of police.

To begin with, Roger, throwing stones to miss, is still conditioned by a distant civilization now in ruins. The old taboo is still just barely effective. Lurking darkly behind a tree, "breathing quickly, his eyelids fluttering" (68), lovingly contemplating the vulnerable littlun, so temptingly defenseless, Roger is a masterly depiction of barely controlled perversion, straight from Ivan Karamazov's analysis of sadism in the chapter called "Rebellion." Even Ralph, decent as he is, is not immune, in the roughhouse of the mock-ritual, from the "sudden, thick excitement" of inflicting pain on a helpless creatures (126). But what is a shocking, fleeting visitation for Ralph is Roger's permanent condition. It is appropriate that, during the killing of the sow-mother with its explicit sexual overtones, he should be the one to find a lodgment for his point and to force it remorselessly "right up her ass!" (150). Who else but the pervert should lead those pursuing the sow, "wedded to her in lust," and, at her death, collapsing "heavy and fulfilled upon her" (149)? Orgasmic release for Roger is always a matter of hurting someone else.

He is a much more frightening figure than Jack, for whereas the latter's cruelty springs from fear—the unfortunate Wilfred is to be beaten because the Chief is angry and afraid (176)—Roger's sadism is the pure, unadulterated thing, with pleasure as its motive. When he hears the delectable news of Wilfred's beating, it breaks upon him like an illumination, and he sits silently savoring the luscious possibilities of irresponsible authority, of unchecked freedom: it is a sadist's Elysium—absolute power and a stock of helpless victims. The officer comes just in time to prevent supplantation, for, as the connoisseur of pain, Roger is already beginning to shoulder the Chief aside to practice his hellish craft. Significantly, the sharpened stick to take Ralph's life is carried by Roger, not Jack. But we do the island an injustice if we blame it for producing Roger; the island merely provides a stage for the talents he brings to it. Roger exhibits the two ostensibly contradictory truths that the book advances: how far the boys have moved away from civilization and what a tiny journey it is. By the close Percy Wemys Madison has completely forgotten the talismanic address chanted throughout to console him in his ordeal—proof at once of how perilously fragile the civilized life is and of how thoroughly effaced it can become. It provokes an alarming question: did we ever truly possess what we so easily forsake?

The speculation is the more fearful because Golding insists throughout on the boys' collective guilt—it is a general inculpation, not simply the arraignment of a few especially wicked individuals. Roger is not a member of some alien species smuggled among us, but a human being, albeit in advanced pathological form: if humanity is sick, he is terminally ill. Nevertheless, his cruelty is that of his species, carried to its ultimate extreme. In *Lord of the Flies* only Simon is immune from the contagion. On the opening pages Ralph plays at being a killer, simulating the fighter plane that blew the boys out of the sky, as he machine-guns Piggy in jest. *Lord of the Flies* shows game turn frighteningly into earnest. Even the mock-ritual, when Robert plays the role of the pig, gets out of hand, and Ralph finds himself battling with the others to inflict pain upon the make-believe victim. The apparent throwaway joke about using a littlun becomes hideous reality when Simon is butchered by the demented boys, still a choir but chanting a very different doxology to a very different god. Significantly, the "good" boys—Ralph, Piggy, Sam, and Eric—participate to the full in the killing of Simon, thus effectively exploding any consoling idea that the wicked, from whom the good are decisively segregated, are wholly to blame for the evil of the world.

All are at fault, big and small alike. When Ralph betrays Piggy over his nickname, "a storm of laughter arose and even the tiniest child joined in. For the moment the boys were a closed circuit of sympathy with Piggy outside" (23). Piggy's bowed head denotes the perennial victim; the double metaphors of storm and circuit leave the children totally without excuse, since their heartlessness stems from nature and civilization alike. Just before his death, Piggy, clinging in blind terror to the narrow ledge and wailing to Ralph not to leave him, becomes the target for the jeering derision of the whole tribe. It is Roger who crushes him with the boulder, but all the boys, save Simon, have tormented him from the first day on the island. Maurice, deliberately trampling the littluns' sand castle, exhibits, to a lesser degree, the same sadistic mentality as Roger, an identical impulse to abuse and to hurt, inhibited only by a parallel fear of chastisement. "There are children of twelve who long to set fire to something. And they do. It's a sort of illness," observes the saintly Alyosha in *The Brothers Karamazov* (682). It is such a malady that Golding investigates in *Lord of the Flies*.

The ubiquity of the ailment is what he is most concerned to impress. "Now the painted group felt the otherness of Samneric, felt the power in their own hands" (198). Again, Dostoyevski is the mentor; no one else has written so illuminatingly on the intoxication of power, or sensed how human beings, stimulated by the headiness of total mastery, can be irresistibly incited to the enactment of the most monstrous atrocities. The most striking confirmation of this universal guilt is supplied by the littlun Henry, himself the object of Roger's unholy desires. At the very moment when Roger is burning to torment him, the oblivious child has trapped some tiny sea-creatures and is "absorbed beyond mere happiness as he felt himself exercising control over living things" (66). Even as the child molester stalks him, the child himself savors that same sense of mastery over other creatures that lies at the root of the sadist's psychology. Golding dramatically demonstrates the distribution of guilt, declining to see cruelty as the monopoly of a perverted few. "In every man, of course, a wild beast is hidden" (*Karamazov*, 283). The universality of the indictment, the throwaway parenthesis tolerating no contradiction: here is Golding's debt to Dostoyevski. Evil is not some outlandish deviation from the human norm: if it is Roger who forces the stake up the sow's anus, it is his companions who laugh uproariously and incriminatingly at the deed.

In *The Brothers Karamazov* the gravamen of Ivan's onslaught on God is the cruelty inflicted on innocent children by adults—simply this, omitting every other evil in creation, justifies Ivan in handing his ticket back, repudiating forever any conceivable eschatological resolution of the world's misery. In *Lord of the Flies* Golding applies an extra turn of the screw: the cruelty inflicted on children is *by* children, and, in a world even more fallen than Dostoyevski's, no one, Simon apart, is innocent—even the smallest child in Golding, if a capacity for cruelty is the test, seems to have eaten the apple. The littluns at play enjoy nothing as much as throwing sand in one another's eyes—they will graduate easily to boulders and, from there, to nuclear missiles. "Schoolchildren are pitiless . . . together, especially at school, they're quite often pitiless" (*Karamazov* 239). One can easily imagine ex-schoolmaster Golding nodding in agreement.

The debt to Dostoyevski is most explicit in Golding's adaptation of "The Legend of the Grand Inquisitor," one of the great peaks in the achievements of Western art and the commanding centre of Dostoyevski's novel. *Lord of the Flies* is a dramatic reenactment, modified to the requirements of a boys' story, of that elemental struggle between freedom and servitude, spirit and power, Christ and Satan, to which Dostoyevski gave canonical form. Simon and Jack are the real options facing the boys in *Lord of the Flies*: climbing the mountain or worshiping the beast—not the altogether lesser, political conflict between Ralph's democratic liberalism and Jack's authoritarianism. Behind Jack and the Grand Inquisitor stand Satan, just as behind Simon stands Christ. When the Grand Inquisitor privately admits to Christ his true allegiance to "the wise and mighty spirit in the wilderness" (*Karamazov*, 295), the spirit who fruitlessly tempted Christ as the Lord of the Flies fruitlessly tempts Simon, he foreshadows Jack's decision to worship the Beast, for Satan and Beelzebub are one. The struggle on the island is between good and evil, and it diminishes the book to see it simply as a contest of warring political systems. Simon facing Jack, like Billy Budd facing Claggart, is the Son of God facing the Evil One; and in all three cases, the hero's crucifixion is the confirmation of his goodness.

From the moment when, introducing himself, Simon "smiled pallidly," he becomes recognizable as belonging to a Christian tradition of pious illness, the antithesis of the choir-leader Jack with his dictatorial ways and manic energy. From Richardson's Clarissa to Henry James's "dove," Milly Threale, sickness and death have been regularly employed to confirm a protagonist's sanctity; Dickens's popularity is another exemplification of the tradition's continuing appeal in the nineteenth century. In *Mansfield Park* Austen provides a particularly provocative example (for which many have still not forgiven her) of sickness as blessed and health as suspect in the contrasting figures of her heroine, Fanny Price, and her adventuress, Mary Crawford—there may be, it seems, a spiritual grace in physical debilitation. But the outstanding example is surely Prince Myshkin, the saintly fool who is the hero of Dostoyevski's novel *The Idiot*, in whom epilepsy is plainly presented as the holy disease.

Golding's Simon (there is no true forerunner for him in *The Coral Island*—he is in every sense, including the Pauline, a new creation) is also an epileptic; when, breaking the choir's ranks, he falls in the fierce sun, Jack contemptuously communicates that he had similar seizures at Gilbraltar and Addis Ababa. Jack, representing the vital principle, the robust and questful body, naturally despises Simon's illness, seeing no good in it, but the reader soon senses that Simon literally falls in the flesh so that he, alone among the boys, will not fall in the spirit. (Asthma is not a holy disease in the sense of epilepsy—asthma prevents Piggy, even had he wished, from becoming a hunter and killer like Jack, and this is surely good, but its value is strictly negative. With Simon, by contrast, there is an unmistakable inference that his ailment is somehow related to his insight into reality, making him see where his healthy companions are blind. It is, doubtless, this element in the character that provokes irritation in certain readers at what strikes them as a reversion to medieval mumbo jumbo).

Dostoyevski can once again be of service in the interpretation of Golding. In a letter to Strakhov he defended Myshkin as character while simultaneously rejecting the charge that his work was not realistic: "Perhaps in the idiot man is more real."[25] In *The Brothers Karamazov* the insufferable schoolboy Kolya condescendingly addresses Alyosha: "I know you are a mystic but—that hasn't put me off. Contact with reality will cure you" (648). Those readers who jib at the character of Simon, finding him strangely unreal and unconvincing, can point to the strong textual support of his companions' opinions of him. Simon is seen by the other boys as "batty" and "nuts," something of an idiot, communing with himself or wandering off alone into the darkness of the forest where no sensible person would ever voluntarily go. At a crucial point in the narrative, it is Simon's "foolish" readiness to traverse the forest alone in the evening to return to Piggy—none of the other boys will risk it—that precipitates the tragedy; had Simon been with the party that climbed the mountain to investigate the beast, there would have been no panic-stricken flight down the slope, for he would have revealed the beast for the poor, decomposing thing it is. It is this apartness, this capacity for words and deeds that the others can only regard as crazy, that makes them neglect and, at times, despise him. Even Ralph, who likes him, is puzzled: "He's queer. He's funny" (59). It is the view that Myshkin's acquaintances take of him, the view carried to a furious extreme by Katerina in *The Brothers Karamazov* when Alyosha says what she does not want to hear: "You're a little religious halfwit—that's what you are!" (223). If not the idiom, this is the sentiment of the boys, Ralph and Piggy included, in *their* indignant response to Simon's idiotic proposal that they should climb the mountain. Their outrage has its origin in a similar aversion to the offensive, unacceptable truth. In all three cases—Myshkin, Alyosha, Simon—it is the person spurned who is the truth-bearer: as determinedly as Dostoyevski, Golding shows that it is the scorned simpleton who is in touch with ultimate reality.

The last thing Golding means us to see in Simon is some vague, woolly minded dreamer, or, worse still, some type of Manichaean whose aversion to matter leads to ascetic withdrawal from an impure world. Simon's "mysticism" has nothing in it of that abhorrence of physical life that the institutional church identified in the Cathars. Fear and distrust of this possibility in mysticism induced the church to establish rules for an approved or allowable mysticism. A "good" mystic must never use contemplation as a pretext for disregarding the common moral duties. His experience, if genuine, strengthens his common virtues of humility, charity, and chastity; it proves to be a diabolic temptation, rather than God's gift, if it breeds hubris, indifference to others, or irregularities of conduct. By their fruits you shall know them: the genuine mystic is a better, not a worse, citizen.

Simon qualifies superbly, passes all the criteria established by the church for "allowable" mysticism. It is no dreamy dropout who walks into the forest "with an air of purpose," first finding fruit for the littluns on the high trees before retreating to his refuge. "Simon. He helps" (59): Ralph simply means this as a tribute to his strange friend's willingness to work while the loafers sidle off to swim and play, but the reader finds a deeper, authorial significance in the words. Simon the helper inevitably evokes Simon of Cyrene, who helped Christ to carry his cross to Calvary. Golding's Simon is equally Christ's auxiliary, within the text. Simon is an even more complex figure than this suggests, but for the purposes of the present argument, especially the relationship between Golding and Dostoyevski, he will be offered as Golding's equivalent of Christ in "The Legend of the Grand Inquisitor."

His prophetic and messianic roles in the book are clearly presented. 'You'll get back to where you came from,' he assures Ralph (122), and although the latter ridicules the promise as irrational, based on mere intuition, a hunch rather than a scientific proof, the conclusion upholds the prophet. "You're batty," retorts Ralph affectionately, recognizing the attempt at consolation, but the book is not designed to exhibit Simon's folly; why, when he talks sense throughout, should he talk piffle now? That his companions consistently misinterpret the sense as folly convicts them, not the speaker. This is most strikingly manifested in Simon's misunderstood message of salvation, vulgarized by Jack, incomprehensible to Piggy: "Maybe it's only us" (97). Look for the beast within, not in some forest creature to be propitiated by Jack, not in the other human being whom Piggy is always so eager to accuse. Simon's message of ubiquitous evil is, paradoxically, one of hope: we are all in the same fallible boat—to confess this is the first, indispensable step toward dealing with it. It is Christ's warning to the Pharisees to fear the pollution within and not the external defilements that can do no hurt to the soul.

"Simon became inarticulate in his effort to expose mankind's essential illness" (97). This is, if we are to believe Golding, the author's own aim in writing *Lord of the Flies*. But it leaves Simon vulnerable to misinterpretation, for Piggy thinks that he's talking about ghosts and Jack about excrement. Nevertheless, Simon is right; it is his despisers who either cannot or will not match his insight into reality.

In his passion and death he becomes most unmistakably a Christ figure. Like Christ, he suffers his temptation in the wilderness—his encounter with the Lord of the Flies, who, in the guise of a "waxy" schoolmaster, attempts to browbeat the boy into submitting to corrupt, adult authority. Again, Golding follows Dostoyevski in showing that the devil who comes to us is bespoke, conceived in familiar terms, the insinuating companion of our experience. No more than with Ivan and his devil in *The Brothers Karamazov* do we know conclusively that this is dialogue and not monologue: the beast is within.

Following his successful resistance to this temptation, self-generated or not, Simon resolves to climb the mountain and face the beast, in a mood reminiscent of Christ at Gethsemane, even to the same idiom of reluctant acceptance: "What else is there to do?" (142). There is here no Nietzschean *amor fati*, no Yeatsian gaiety overcoming the dread: the cup must be drunk simply because it is the Father's will and there is no alternative. Elation, even confidence, are noticeably absent. Simon drearily, dutifully forces himself to climb the mountain and by the end of his *via dolorosa* the child staggers on like an old man. Unless you become as little children; here the movement is in the contrary direction, from childhood to senescence. When he "hid his face, and toiled on," there are echoes of plucking out the eye that gives scandal: better march blind toward the beast than flee down the hillside with perfect vision (161). For he that loses his life will save it. Simon's life is saved, his courage rewarded, when he sees the poor "beast" that struck panic into the other boys. Jack, who despises Simon as a sick fool, treats the living with contempt; it is the mystic who treats even the dead with reverence, freeing the poor body, that should be rotting away, from the wind's indignity. Even a killer from the sky, now himself a corpse, deserves courtesy. Only then, the release accomplished, does Simon start back down the hill with the good news of salvation that must be communicated to his berserk companions. In the crucifixion that waits at the end of his journey, the final, irrefutable parallel with Christ is established. The sacrificial victim's dying cry about a dead man on a hill, an unmistakable allusion to Golgotha, simply highlights what no reader should, in any case, fail to see.

As Simon the messianic, so Jack as clearly represents the satanic principle. Simon's resistance to the Lord of the Flies emphasizes the capitulation of his companions, a capitulation that conforms precisely to the Grand Inquisitor's exposition in his diatribe against Christ. The boys' fall into servitude replicates the etiology of enslavement advanced by the Inquisitor: freedom abused, then gratefully discarded in return for security and bread. Ivan's account of the flight from freedom speaks directly to events on the island: "I suppose men themselves are to blame: they were given paradise, they wanted freedom and they stole the fire from heaven, knowing perfectly well that they would become unhappy, so why should we pity them?" (*Karamazov*, 285). Only 22 years separate *The Coral Island* (1858) from *The Brothers Karamazov* (1880), but Dostoyevski engages Golding like a contemporary, while Ballantyne's is another world.

The Inquisitor disagrees with Ivan: he pities men—for him the culprit is Christ. The gravamen of the charge against Christ is his wild overestimation of man's capacity for freedom—as well send a child into a magazine with a box of matches. In giving men the ruinous freedom that is the cause of all their woe, Christ, however unintentionally, became the foe of man. The Inquisitor, as man's true lover, gives man what he both wants and needs: not freedom but safety. It is a kindness to take freedom away from its abusers, since "nothing has been more unendurable to man and to human society than freedom" (*Karamazov*, 296). Freedom is an injury to the weaklings to whom it has been so maladroitly given. The Inquisitor's image of men as foolish, rebellious schoolboys is that chosen by Golding for his own dark parable: "They are little children rioting in class and driving out their teacher. But an end will come to the transports of the children, too. They will pay dearly for it. . . . But they will realise at last, the foolish children, that although they are rebels, they are impotent rebels who are unable to keep up with their rebellion" (*Karamazov*, 300). They will crawl back to teacher, begging to be chastised and disciplined. The Inquisitor refers, of course, to his own dictatorship, which will arise in response to the plea of these frantic creatures to be saved from themselves: the kingdom of secure servitude that will replace Christ's blunder of enfranchisement.

It is the argument embodied in Jack, though it is undercut by Golding's text. Golding had just lived through a war in which a leader, very much in Jack's mold and an exponent of the Inquisitor's authoritarianism, had killed himself in a Berlin bunker after leading his nation to total and bloody defeat. The guarantee of security in exchange for freedom is a fraud, as the boys would have discovered had rescue not arrived. Golding's children escape rather than expel their teacher, and under Jack they set the island to the torch. Golding is in no mood to be taken in by the Inquisitor's rhetoric in the middle of the twentieth century or by his specious alternatives of ruinous freedom or secure servitude—under Hitler the servitude was ruinous. And so Golding offers his own alternatives: human responsibility or total destruction. But, however specious the Inquisitor's logic, Golding knows, too, how powerfully seductive it was and still is to the beleagured denizens of the twentieth century—how else can we explain the rise of the dictators in our time? "We have corrected your great work and have based it on miracle, mystery and authority" (*Karamazov*, 301). Reprimand and claim alike continue to reverberate in the annals of twentieth-century history, and Jack, pursuing the same program, is a fitting son of the Grand Inquisitor.

He is often misinterpreted as a lover of savage disorder, when he is really an advocate of stern totalitarian discipline. Far from disliking rules, he loves them, too much and for the wrong reason: "We'll have rules! he cried excitedly. 'Lots of rules! Then when anyone breaks 'em . . .' " (36). Those critics who find the book upholding Augustine against Pelagius should reflect that Jack is a confirmed Augustinian with a zest for retribution. From the outset his authoritarianism is glaringly evident. He rages against the democratic procedures of the assembly; the way to get things done, he believes, is to compel, not ask, to terrorize, not persuade. "I say this": under Jack the diktat replaces the debate. "The Chief has spoken": what need for further discussion? (155). That is why it is such a disastrous concession when Ralph, to appease his mortified rival, assigns him control of the choir. Jack, as leader of the hunters, becomes invincible as lord of the feast. The need to hunt and kill entails the formation of an army and hence the undermining of the democratic process by this rival power structure. Ralph's bitterness in lashing the hunters for throwing away the chance of rescue should include an element of self-chastisement.

Nor does Ralph emerge with credit from his showdown with Jack, for he finds the lure of meat as irresistible as anyone else. His resolve to refuse the meat, so dearly obtained, crumbles and he is soon gnawing as voraciously as the others. It is a decisive moment for Jack, as his triumphant cry proclaims, "I got you meat" (80).

This is not, as is sometimes mistakenly said, a slide from society into savagery—rather the replacement of one kind of society by another. Jack's exultant boast is the announcement of a new totalitarian contract in which freedom is the forfeit of meat. Ralph, puzzled and distressed because the boys prefer Jack to himself, would have known the answer had he read Dostoyevski instead of Ballantyne. The Grand Inquisitor (who was certainly not advocating a return to nature) declared that man will worship the provider of bread, and Jack does even better by providing roast pork. Again, Ballantyne is subverted: in *The Coral Island* the boys convert the cannibals by giving them roast pork; in *Lord of the Flies* the same dish is the means of corruption. The Inquisitor, who condemns Christ for refusing the devil's temptation to turn stones into bread, using food to buy obedience, would have applauded Jack. The provision of meat becomes a key element in the establishment of autocracy. The democrats can stay and get diarrhea with Ralph, or defect to Jack and a full table, at the trifling cost of their freedom. The meat-giver wins hands down: a hungry democracy cannot compete with a well-fed tyranny—the boys are transformed into slaves, not savages.

Even Ralph and Piggy, fine principles notwithstanding, are driven by hunger toward Jack's camp, where he sits, "painted and garlanded . . . like an idol," upon his log-throne, by merit raised to that bad eminence, undisputed lord of the feast (164).[26] Contemptuously, he allows the shamefaced pair to eat, and Piggy, "betrayed by his stomach . . . stooped for more." The verbs exactly convey the fall inherent in the action. When, later, the quarrel rekindles and Ralph attacks the tribe for running after meat, Jack only needs to point to the accusatory bone in Ralph's hand: you cannot deplore a robbery and share in the loot. It is analogous to that devastating moment in *Nineteen Eighty-four* when O'Brien explodes Winston's claim to moral superiority by simply playing back the incriminating tape on which the "good" man promises to commit the very atrocities that he denounces in Big Brother (214). In each case, the compromised hero has forfeited the right to condemn his opponent.

"So they stood and ate beneath a sky of thunderous brass that rang with the storm-coming" (165). The heightened, evocative language, the compressed gravity of that final coinage, impress the crucial significance of the act, comparable to Eve's eating of the apple in book 9 of *Paradise Lost*. The culprit who should have been condemned for neglecting the fire has become the chief, not despite, but because of his dereliction: "I got you meat." It confirms Jack as dictator, confirms, too, the accuracy of the Grand Inquisitor's account of the riddance of freedom.

Miracle, mystery, authority: these are the Grand Inquisitor's amendments to the ruinous freedom of Christ, and Jack supplies the mystery as effectively as he does the authority. Posing as the disciple of Christ, the Inquisitor is really the servant of Satan. Jack, leader of the choir, similarly becomes the priest of Beelzebub, and his new religion of devil-worship, with its rites and rituals, doxologies and propitiations, brings comfort to its followers, a sense of placating the power that rules the island. Only in the element of miracle does the parallel break down; Jack is no thaumaturge. Killing pigs may be a surrender to Satan, but it is not as miraculous as turning stones into bread or casting oneself unhurt from the temple would have been had Christ similarly surrendered. But the miracle is still present, brilliantly transferred from Jack to the deus ex machina of the rescuing officer. We smile at the miracle in Ballantyne when the boys are saved from apparently unavoidable destruction by the conversion of the savages to Christianity—how splendidly and ludicrously convenient. But the miracle in Golding is only superficially less absurd and is totally irrelevant to the deeper concerns of the fable. The miraculous rescue of the boys will not be replicated in the case of men; not the Grand Inquisitor but Dostoyevski's Christ is vindicated by *Lord of the Flies*. There is no salvation in miracle or mystery or authority—there is only freedom and the awesome responsibility to use it well.

The greatness of Golding's book is that it presents this challenge, not in any spirit of sunny assurance or glib euphoria, but heavy with a sense of the perilously problematic resolution of the issue. Threat rather than salvation is the burden of the text, as its last great echo of Dostoyevski makes clear. As Ralph flees for his life on the burning island, "a herd of pigs came squealing out of the greenery . . . and rushed away into the forest" (219). It is a striking reverberation of the passage taken from Luke's Gospel by Dostoyevski to serve as epigraph for his great novel of revolutionary madness and collective mania, *The Devils*. In Dostoyevski and Golding alike, it is the human beings, not the pigs, that are possessed; in the souls of men and boys the Gadarene demons are housed, and the blind rush to destruction seems unstoppable. How to exorcise the demons: this is the problem that *Lord of the Flies* poses but does not solve.

6

Janus's Island

Writing when the century had run exactly half its course and four years before *Lord of the Flies* was published, Hannah Arendt, in the preface to *The Origins of Totalitarianism*, divided mankind into two opposed but equally mistaken groups: "those who believe in human omnipotence (who think that everything is possible if one knows how to organise masses for it) and those for whom powerlessness has become the major experience of their lives."[1] This division, in her view, augured ill for our survival as a species: balanced judgment and measured insight, the qualities she desiderates, are unlikely to flourish alongside "desperate hope and desperate fear," however much these may seem to match the bleak annals of twentieth-century history. She cautions against surrender to either delusion: "The central events of our time are not less effectively forgotten by those committed to a belief in an unavoidable doom, than by those who have given themselves up to reckless optimism" (Arendt, vii). Accordingly, her declared purpose in writing the book was to expose simultaneously these equally erroneous reactions to modern history: "Progress and Doom are two sides of the same medal, . . . both are articles of superstition, not of faith" (Arendt, vii). She might easily have condemned them in harsher terms, for, traditionally, they are not merely superstitions but sins, the two great primal offenses from which all other transgressions flow. What she calls progress and doom had long been known to the Christian centuries as presumption and despair.

Do not presume—one of the thieves was damned; do not despair—one of the thieves was saved. Although the advice is at once sensible and salutary, the evidence suggests that human beings find it difficult, if not impossible, to avoid succumbing to one of these opposing errors; more striking still, they seem to escape the one only as prelude to falling into the other. We are devotees of the pendulum, swinging between extremes, apparently incapable of the total, the comprehensive view. We are the heirs of Polyphemus, the cyclops's children; we lack the saving bifocalism, the dual vision, that would prevent us from falling prey to either extreme. Yet truth is binary; unless we see double, we see false. If we look in the mirror and see only what is noble and beautiful, then the mirror is a cheat, reflecting, at best, a partial—an incomplete—truth; if the mirror unfailingly assures us that we are the fairest of all, then it flatters and presumption is not far away.

But despair is not the cure for presumption, simply its equally misguided opposite. If the mirror reflects only what is vile and sordid— if we see only the face of the Yahoo or the bag of filth of *Nineteen Eighty-four*—this is also distortion, though now it produces disgust rather than delight, shame rather than elation. It is so easy to slip from a facile self-overestimation to an equally harmful self-devaluation. How to acknowledge the Yahoo in the self without surrendering to despair; how to applaud the nobility in man, "the beauty of the world! the paragon of animals,"[2] without being undermined by vanity: this is the problem. To see true we must look twice; only a double mirror can correct our moral astigmatism.

Frustrating this is the inveterate human tendency to cherish the single vision, to cosset exclusive and particular interpretations intolerant of alternative exegesis. We exalt "either-or" above "both-and," and thereby we fall into the competing blunders of excessive self-esteem or self-misprision. Achieving and maintaining the right balance—how testing it is. Thus, Marlowe's Faustus, the scientific libertine who gains control over nature while losing control over himself, speaks pertinently to our predicament. It is not only that his unbridled search for forbidden knowledge serves as an admonition against modern man's equally perverted ingenuity, which threatens to reduce the planet to radioactive ash; crucial as the theme of forbidden knowledge is, of still more fundamental relevance is the psychological development of Faustus, for this is what ensures his destruction.

Toward the close of Marlowe's play, in one last evasion of the truth, Faustus blames scholarship for his fall: "Oh, would I had never seen Wittenberg, never read book!" (83). It is unjust to fault the university for his abuse of learning or to condemn books because he perverts them. The last, desperate attempt to dodge damnation comes with the foolishly futile promise "I'll burn my books," but such incendiarism is totally irrelevant except on the untenable assumption that nescience is salvation, that to be wilfully ignorant is to be secure. Our modern technology need not destroy us, provided we are its masters and not its slaves. What must be avoided is the fatalistic capitulation to technology as autonomous, with a will of its own greater than the will that invented it, and invested with a self-generating momentum that humankind can neither regulate nor suspend. This would, indeed, complete our ominous identification with Faustus, for despair, not scholarship, damns him—a despair that is the ineluctable consequence of an earlier presumption: resigning himself to his doom, he guarantees its occurrence. The landscape of Faustus's mind as he moves from presumption to despair is at the core of the play's relevance to our present condition.

In this short, brilliantly dramatic text, Marlowe anticipates Hannah Arendt's analysis of the modern predicament. His hero enacts in a single life the crisis of contemporary culture. The play has been described as the spiritual autobiography of an age, but it speaks prophetically to our own times. Faustus begins in rebellion, against the limitations of the human: what use to be master of medicine if it does not make you the lord of death, if you still cannot command the graves to open? "Yet art thou still but Faustus and a man" (7). It is an existential dilemma: how is Faustus to justify his being? One by one he summons the disciplines already subdued, rejecting each as unworthy of his high ambition, incommensurate with his exalted conception of the self. The search for an endeavor equal to this heroic view of man leads him inevitably to necromancy, forbidden knowledge, since, in this grandiose scenario, anticipating Nietzsche, man can realize his true potential only by challenging God and defying taboo. Man must become his own god or live on in timid, disgraceful servitude. "A sound magician is a mighty God" (8): it is the solicitation of the tempter in Eden—"you shall be as Gods"—the only difference being that Faustus tempts himself.

It is this discontent with the datum of the human that makes Faustus Satan's follower. *Non serviam*: like Lucifer, Faustus regards it as demeaning to be in any sense limited or circumscribed, subject to any constraint. Satan proposes a release from medieval bonds. The diabolic contract springs from an exasperation with limits and an unbounded confidence in man's autonomy, the sense of omnipotence referred to by Arendt: Faustus embraces it in a mood of euphoric

expectation. The contrast with the shivering wretch of the play's conclusion is both striking and shocking. Gone is the cockiness of his
younger self. "Hell's a fable" had been his frivolously irresponsible
retort when Mephistophilis, a scrupulously honest devil, attempted to
convey the inexpressible torment of the place (28). Now, as the clock
sprints toward midnight, there is no more time for levity. Hell is
now inescapable reality and its erstwhile derider, who once aspired to
godhead, now longs in vain to be a drop of water or a clod of earth—
things far below man in the scale of creation, but enviable because
they cannot be damned: "Why wert thou not a creature wanting soul?"
(88). The wish now is not to rise above his station but to sink far
below it. What reduces the humanist hero to envy of inanimate matter
is his pessimistic conviction that hell is unavoidable. Faustus swings
from one erroneous extreme to another, from hubristic self-exaltation
to an equally excessive self-deprecation. Santayana thought that Marlowe was dramatizing Calvinist predestination, depicting a protagonist
who sins and tries to repent but is prevented from doing so. But the
text, properly understood, will not sustain this interpretation. If, finally, Faustus cannot repent, it is for the soundly orthodox reason that
he has capitulated to despair, to Arendt's sense of powerlessness—the
sin that is the predictable outcome of his initial offense of presumption.

That he is guilty of presumption is undeniable. Thinking of the
end to which his misconduct may bring him, he consoles himself with a
highly selective, one-eyed manipulation of the gospel evidence: "Tush,
Christ did call the thief upon the cross; then rest thee, Faustus, quiet
in conceit" (68). But one of the thieves was damned. This crassly facile
assumption of a guaranteed deathbed reprieve is a monstrous devalua-
tion of the good thief's heroism—here, surely, was one last-minute repentance that did *not* come easy. His companion, who put the perfectly
natural demand to be taken down from the cross, did not receive a
similar promise of paradise. It isn't as easy as Faustus (and we) think.

Yet the idea that we can ring for salvation as for room service
persists in the presumers, among whom we may include Heine—"*Dieu
me pardonerra, c'est son métier*"—and Omar Khayyam:

> They talk of some strict Testing
> of us—Pish!
> He's a Good Fellow and 'twill
> all be well.[3]

The delusion that last-minute amendment is easy, that the habits of a
lifetime can be casually repudiated in the very moment of impending

dissolution, seems rooted in our nature. Yet so, too, paradoxically, is the counteridea that everything is a bad business, hopelessly beyond reprieve or amendment, that there is nothing we can do save wait for the blow to fall. If ever we believed that contrition is easy, Faustus himself, the great presumer, would prove the contrary. Knowing that death is imminent, that one drop of Christ's blood is enough to save him, that, most conclusively of all, he need only cry out for mercy for it to be given, he nevertheless cannot do it: "I do repent and yet I do despair. . . . Sweet friends, what shall become of Faustus, being in hell forever?" (84). His despair is the natural terminus of his initial exorbitant expectations—no one is more vulnerable to disillusion than he who expects too much.

Wrong when he presumes and wrong when he despairs, deceived at each self-destructive extreme—Faustus's career provides a template for the wayward history of our times. His twenty-four-year passage from exuberant young scholar to aging wretch provides a perfect paradigm for the sharp transition from nineteenth-century optimism to twentieth-century despair, from a sense of great expectations to apprehensions of unprecedented disaster: "False and absurd doctrines, when exposed, have a natural tendency to beget scepticism in those who received them without reflection. None are so likely to believe too little as those who have begun by believing too much"[4] It would be as superficially foolish to reject the relevance of Faustus simply because hell is no longer our terror as to reject the relevance of *The Alchemist* because alchemy is no longer our pursuit. Our own Faustian predilection for the pendulum is manifest in the swing from the redemptive literature of the last century to the accusatory literature of today.

The animus of backlash, the element of retaliation, are unmistakable in modern literature: there is a manifest resolve to be revenged for having been the dupes of a discredited mythos, a sentimental cheat. The intention is at once punitive and revocatory: to chastise culprits and to rescind false doctrine. Pelagius has taken a beating, much of it deserved, in our own dark, Augustinian days. One understands only too well the reason for such a turnabout: it is the revenge of reality upon failed utopia, the anger of those who have reached the promised land only to discover the fraud of the prospectus, and who instinctively demand that the place be razed to the ground: disappointed dreamers make implacable foes.

Yet, as always, there is a danger of reacting too fiercely in the opposite direction, converting every image of hope into one of despair, repudiating brightness to embrace gloom. Where is the gain in cartwheeling from utopian humanism to a fixation on depravity, from paradise too cheaply obtained to paradise irremediably lost, from presumption to despair? Is it surprising that our calculations continue erroneous when we have simply changed every plus into a minus? There is, of course, no way back, even if we wished, to the inadequate, one-eyed mythos of the preceding century. We cannot wish the works of the dark epiphany unwritten, however chill and disturbing they be. Their value is precisely this: they make it impossible for us to cling to discredited myth, they force us to reappraise our condition against the irrefutable facts of contemporary life. Whether the master be Conrad, Mann, Orwell, Camus, or Golding, whether the setting be the heart of darkness, plague-stricken Venice, the London of Airstrip One, the Dantean circles of Amsterdam, or Beelzebub's island, there is the same moment of dismayed discovery, the same revelation of self-pollution. Self-knowledge is almost a synonym for self-contempt. If our condition seems no different from that of the doomed Faustus, neither is our destination: "Why, this is hell, nor am I out of it" (19).

Salvation depends upon self-love, but the right kind of self-love is a heroic enterprise. The works of the dark epiphany, reflecting the history of our time, have made it difficult for man, resisting planned degradation, to fall back upon the fact of his own goodness. How can man both know and love himself? It is the most important moral question of our time and it will require all our patience and ingenuity to solve it.

"Ah, this dear old planet! All is clear now. We know ourselves; we now know of what we are capable" (Camus, 35). The voice is that of Camus's sneering mudslinger in *The Fall*, and the malevolently gloating tone makes it plain that this knowledge is irrevocably incriminating, shattering the myth of our innocence beyond recall. Jean-Baptiste Clamence is the pendulum man par excellence, beginning by loving himself and his fellows too easily and too ignorantly, ending by dispraising them to deplorable excess. One partial truth is replaced by another, the single eye that shone so fondly now glowers in dark disapproval. Polyphemus is bound to get it wrong, at one extreme or another; only two-eyed men can see the whole truth. Never has this gift of a blessed bifocalism been more urgently required than in our own atrocity-benumbed century, exposed as we have been to the single, destructive truth, peculiar to our times, that man is shabby, unreliable, and vile, and that "this is all according to the due course of things" (Swift, *Gulliver*, 345). But it is hazardous to know only one truth: men who see only their frailties become addicts, men who resignedly accept that it is all according to the due course of things will have no motive to act otherwise. We must see twice to see true.

Bifocalism means seeing what the age tends to ignore, and our age has been all too understandably obsessed with the dark, destructive side of human nature. Sir Michael Tippett has argued that the task of the artist is to bring to the world the images that it lacks, reminding a chaotic world of harmony and a violent world of peace. This chapter presents Golding as such as artist, one of those few writers in our time gifted with the ability to take the salutary double view, to see with Sir Thomas Browne that man is "that great and true Amphibium, whose nature is disposed to live, not onely like other creatures in divers elements, but in divided and distinguished worlds"[5]; to recognize with Pope that man is "the glory, jest and riddle of the world"[6]; to acknowledge with Pascal that "man's condition is dual ... that unless we realise the duality of human nature we remain invincibly ignorant of the truth about ourselves" (Pensées, 65); to insist with Herman Melville that "the tortoise is both black and bright."[7] Life is binary, duplex; that is why Joyce, with unerring insight, chose for his nationalist fanatic Polyphemus, the one-eyed man who sees only the single truth that guarantees overall distortion.

That is also why Simon is so affirmative a figure in *Lord of the Flies*, the one but all-important shaft of light in an otherwise dark text. Even on Beelzebub's island, among sadists and savages, Simon continues to see the doubleness of man. When he thinks of the human being, it is of a creature at once heroic and sick. He rejects any false segregation into elect and reprobate; the beast is us, a general incrimination with no exemptions. He is not encouraging surrender to the beast, simply the need to know where it lives so that we can control it. Maybe it's us, he tentatively proposes, and the other boys, with Piggy leading the chorus, howl him down in indignant derision. But he is proved horribly right when the tribe, with both Piggy and Ralph to the fore, kill him: who can doubt any longer where the beast lives? Simon's wisdom is to see that the beast is *in* us but is not *wholly* us; if we were not double, our case would indeed be hopeless. Simon alone offers hope because only he can internalize the beast; only he, with his double vision, can master this insight. It is the single perspective that leads to shipwreck. In duplicity is salvation; we are, blessedly, double agents. Simon confronts the beast with the unevasive words of Prospero appropriating Caliban: "this thing of darkness I acknowledge mine."[8] Piggy, angry and shocked, repudiates all relationship. The works of the dark epiphany are not to be spurned as slanderous untruths. But the admission of guilt, provided it does not stupefy, is our best defense: how can we be broken by what we have already confessed? The Lord of the Flies attempts, vainly, to bully Simon into submission by telling him that everything is a bad business, but Simon is not to be cowed by what he already knows.

Yet, as the text makes indisputably clear, everything is not just a bad business. On the contrary, as Simon himself sees, everything is double—the island belongs to Janus, not Beelzebub, though Beelzebub, understandably, would have us believe otherwise. It is especially important to recognize this because Golding entices us into partial judgments of the meaning of his work, fostering readings not so much wrong as unbalanced. However plausible, they require, at a deeper level of discrimination, those adversarial and competing interpretations without which misreading is inevitable. Among such misreadings is the presentation of *Lord of the Flies* as a "tory" text upholding order against freedom, civilization against nature, the regulated polis against a jungle free-for-all. Cognate is the belief that Golding regards nature as irredeemably evil, a fallen world that owns Beelzebub as lord; in this view, man's only hope is to be rescued from nature, his own included, as the hagridden children are plucked from the jungle by the emissary of adult society. At an extreme, Golding is endowed with a Manichaean sensibility that damns nature and culture, jungle and city, alike, as beyond redemption: man is nature's excrement, the animal forsaken by Gulliver as hopeless, the bag of filth that Winston contemplates in the mirror. Support for these views can doubtless be recruited from the pages of Golding's text; what is equally true is that they can be maintained only by ignoring countervailing evidence that is just as weighty.

Here is the clue to the uniqueness of the book. It is a text in which everything appears twice, in radically opposed versions of reality, contradictory yet complementary—and this applies not only to its subject matter, its views of man and nature, but also to its style, with its competing narratologies of schoolboy slang and narrator's gloss. This doubleness alone would identify Simon as the tale's interpreter and savior, since only he possesses the bifocalism to see true: in the realm of Polyphemus, Simon sees double. The myopic Piggy, by contrast, is soon literally one-eyed, becoming in fact what he has always metaphorically been; while Ralph, so touchingly direct, is confused and unnerved at the strange doubleness of things: "If faces were different when lit from above or below—what was a face? What was anything?" (85). This bewilderment is fatal in a text that insists you see twice to see true. Man is both heroic and sick: to miss either is to go astray, as

Ralph does. "What makes things break up like they do?" (154). The plea is the more piteous in being addressed to Piggy, as bemused as himself beneath his shallow rationalist confidence. Simon could have told him; as the Lord of the Flies acknowledges in his duel with Simon (Golding's recapitulation of the wilderness encounter of Christ and Satan), Simon has intuited the truth of things.

Ralph is baffled because of his Polyphemic vision. Simon, by contrast, is saddened but not stunned by Jack: if man is sick, Jack is an extreme case, to be cured if possible, but not to be cowered from in incredulous dismay. What good is a doctor who is petrified of disease? It is Piggy who dogmatically insists that we have doctors for everything, and so we do. The irony is that he fails to recognize Simon as the only healer for the island's ills. Simon is the true physician because of his dual vision, and the text demands such a hero if only because of the remarkably double way in which it is written.

The boys—how could it be otherwise?—lack a language commensurate with the intensity of their emotions, whether of anticipation, delight, or dread. *Lord of the Flies* is, in a sense, a work of translation, from the pucrile idiom of prep school to a discourse of mature significance, relying heavily upon the narrator to effect this transition. Only he can remedy the recurring deficiencies of perception and articulation, giving tongue to what would otherwise be trivial, exalting an unpleasant adventure story into a parable of profound and universal import. The book exhibits a dual response, children's and narrator's, to a dual nature, beautiful and menacing.

The struggle to scale the mountain is rewarded at the top by a stunningly beautiful panoramic view, which the narrator takes it upon himself to convey. Ralph's shining eyes as he turns to his equally entranced companions make plain the ecstasy of exploration and discovery, but this can only be verbally communicated in the impoverished idiom of childhood: "Wacco. . . . Wizard. . . . Smashing. . . . Golly!" (28, 29, 30). Such are the boyish equivalents of the "Immortality Ode" or a hymn to natural beauty by Hopkins. The narrator must come to the rescue with a second language, a remedial discourse, which redeems the poverty of schoolboy jargon. The description of what the boys see comes from the narrator's pen: "the lip of a cirque," the "blue flower" that "spilled lavishly among the canopy of the forest," the air dense with butterflies, and, encompassing all, the great circumscribing ocean (30). The boys patently lack the linguistic and emotional resources to make such beauty palpably, textually present.

The view from the mountain is one of those striking moments in Golding—we scour Swift in vain for anything similar—celebrating the beauty of creation, and it is the narrator, inevitably in a text whose oldest character is twelve, who provides these hymnlike passages. Wordsworth may delude himself about the child being a mighty philosopher, a seer blest; ex-schoolmaster Golding knows that the rapture would be expressed as "wizard" and "golly." This linguistic and aesthetic rescue, the artist's rescue of the tale from the emotional and verbal puerility of its actors, is the paramount rescue in the book.

There are two parallel texts, the first in a "low" style of schoolboy slang evocative of the world of Greyfriars and Billy Bunter, the other in the "high" style of the narrator's gloss and commentary, his reinterpretation of the action to reveal its underlying import. Each text has its own recognizable imagery. Ralph, seeing the seabirds on the rock, exclaims "Like icing . . . on a pink cake," and the boyish simile is instinctively appropriate (27). But when we read that "far below his armpit he saw the luminous flowering round the rock," we know that Ralph saw no such thing, for the metaphor is not his but the narrator's (207). It is a kind of literary prestidigitation in which the reader is happily and pleasingly deceived. Who would rather read that Ralph had tears in his eyes than that "the vivid stars were split and danced all ways" (207)?

Without the narrator's commentary, we would be depressingly restricted to the dulled perceptions or incomprehensions of the children. The littlun Percival, surrendering to floods of tears, is depicted as a minuscule Christ, the child of sorrows, nailed to his grief like a crucifixion. He stands for something the children could not possibly know, the homelessness of man: "a sorrow that was universal" (95). Behind Percival is the perennial human sense of loss and exile, the abandonment of Pascal, the *Geworfenheit* of Heidegger—but the child weeps without knowing why; an adult exegesis is impressed upon a childish experience.

The narrator is always poised to resume a control which he may temporarily have abandoned for dramatic effect. He knows, for example, that it is the savior Simon who staggers out of the forest into the maddened circle, but he adopts the perspective of the demented boys to describe it as the coming of the beast—then, suddenly, in midaction he startlingly switches to show the tribe as the true beast, with Simon its victim (168). Even when the boys say things that make perfect sense in the limited context of their immediate application, the reader sometimes intuits a deeper, authorial significance, with the everyday words appropriated for a purpose beyond their first intention. Ralph explodes in anger when the imperiled boys dally to play childish games: "We want smoke. And you go wasting your time. You roll rocks"

(18). The supreme example of such futile activity is Sisyphus, but *he* was condemned to hell, doomed, choiceless. To choose to be Sisyphus, to prefer play to rescue, strikes Ralph as criminal folly, and when the rock rolling finally becomes murder, we see that the children are as much in hell as their great original.

A striking instance of this double narratology occurs when Jack, fuming at Ralph's rebuke over the dead fire, turns upon Piggy and beats him. It is a banal, an everyday event—the school bully beating the school butt, Piggy getting his daily dose like thousands of children all over the country. A third child goes, unremarkably, to the victim's assistance, and the narrator suddenly and startlingly raises the commonplace incident to the level of high tragedy: "Passions beat about Simon on the mountain-top with awful wings" (78). The reader catches his breath at the astonishing transition from a playground rumpus to the elementally primitive world of the *The Bacchae*. That the narrator alone can bring out the fearful significance of these otherwise childish goings-on is made clear when Ralph condemns Jack for the attack: "That was a dirty trick" (78). As a judgment on what has occurred this is bathetic, simply a little boy grousing over a dead fire and an injured chum; it is the narrator's intervention that prevents us from taking so inadequately humdrum a view.

"Passion, and passion in its profoundest, is not a thing demanding a palatial stage whereon to play its part. Down among the groundlings, among the beggars and rakers of the garbage, profound passion is enacted. And the circumstances that provoke it, however trivial or mean, are no measure of its power" (Melville, 356). Melville's impassioned plea for the democratization of tragedy, as he wrests it from the hands of the hitherto privileged aristocrat, is pertinent as Golding audaciously extends the claim to children, but it takes all the high resources of his art to make the claim good.

The most riveting incongruity or doubleness of all is that between the boys' words and their deeds, between the idiom of prep school and the actions of hell—laughter and insanity, Billy Bunter and chums transplanted to the world of de Sade and Auschwitz. This must surely rank as one of the great tours-de-force of modern fiction. Conrad had shown in *Heart of Darkness* how atrocity can consort with culture; Golding shows it cohabiting with childhood, and a childhood retaining its puerile and retarded tongue. There is a constant oscillation between Greyfriars and nightmare. "I'm not going to play any longer. Not with you" (140). Jack, thwarted, blubbers like a crybaby and goes off in a sulk—but he is a lethal crybaby who will turn the playground into a charnel. His words are, after all, essentially what Lucifer once said to

God, and Jack evokes his master in this odd mélange of tantrums and terror—Satan, too, is a spoiled child. 'See, clever?' (166). It is the puerile idiom of schoolyard taunting, but the speaker is as fearful on the island as Stalin in the Kremlin or Caligula in Rome. "Stop being silly!" (193). Ralph's rebuke highlights the astonishing mismatch of words and deeds—one might think some peccadillo were in question: a door ajar, inane horseplay; how inappropriate it sounds when addressed to a guard in Auschwitz or a torturer in Chile. No wonder that "the tribe of painted savages giggled" when Ralph complains that they aren't "playing the game," as though he were reprimanding the cricketers of Greyfriars instead of the killers of Piggy and Simon (196)—and yet "giggled" inevitably takes us back to the world of pillow fights and midnight feasts.

Repeatedly, the hopelessly inadequate schoolboy slang is used to describe the deeds of hell—it is a contagion that spreads to the Lord of the Flies himself. "They're going to do you," he warns Simon, and the horrific slaughter that follows shows all too clearly what the euphemism entails (159). "I'm going to get waxy": it is an exasperated schoolmaster cautioning a wayward child rather than a psychopath about to explode (159). Nowhere is this ludicrous linguistic deficiency better exhibited than when the twins, Samneric, are seized and bound by the savages on Jack's orders. They protest against the violation "out of the heart of civilization," and this is the apogee of their outrage: "Oh, I say. . . . Honestly!" (198). It is a triumph of understatement: someone has left dirty socks in a washbasin. Ralph, being hunted to death, grasps foolishly at a schoolboy formula to exorcise the demons, foiling his pursuers with the talismanic declaration, "I've got pax" (205). Even when he faces the terrible truth of his predicament, the childishness survives as he racks his mind on how "to diddle the savages" (211). Verb and noun jar in an incongruous blend of child's play and butchery, gamesmanship and cannibalism. "One for his nob! Give him a fourpenny one!" (81). The boyish knockabout of the slang after the killing of the first pig, far from disguising, calls attention to the horror enacted and to the gust of sadism that has swept through the first form. The doubleness of the text is exhibited in this juxtaposition of word and deed, the vocabulary of boyhood and the adult action performed.

As with style, so with content: there is discernible throughout *Lord of the Flies* a recurring contrast of episodes and characters, an echoing of earlier events in circumstances diametrically different. Everything is twofold, every perspective provokes a competing alternative. Man, in Simon's unerring insight, is both heroic and sick. The dead parachutist is harmless and horrible, a loathsome corpse that must, nevertheless, be treated with respect. Faces seen from above are strangely different from faces seen from below, a truth that unnerves Ralph, who would have things conveniently single. The choirboys are killers, the rationalist Piggy is lazy, the decent Ralph experiences bloodlust. There are two logs, the democratic bench of the liberal assembly and the throne of Jack's Asiatic court. Jack's satanic dance has its obverse in the innocent dance of the butterflies. There are two radically contrasted ingestions: Simon, losing consciousness, falls into the beast's mouth in what is a type of mythic death and resurrection, going down into darkness, like Christ or Orpheus, in order to emerge again into life and light (159); Jack, however, swallowed whole by the beast, becomes part of it: "He tried to convey the compulsion to track down and kill that was *swallowing* him up" (55; my italics).

These are the strategies and techniques of poetry rather than of realistic fiction, operating through thematic and imagistic reverbera- tion, as in that hair-raising description, like the enactment of some weird prophecy in *Macbeth*, of the corpse that "trod with ungainly feet the tops of the high trees" (169)—the dead parachutist who literally becomes an air-man. It is a poetic world of contraries and tensions: the miraculous throbbing stars and the snapping sharks beyond the reef belong, incredibly, to the same creation, as do Blake's lamb and tiger. Jack, like Milton's Satan, is brave and bad; Simon the server confronts Roger the sadist. Simon called Peter is the rock of Christ, but Beelzebub, too, has his rock, in the crevice of which Jack fixes the stick with its impaled head in tribute to the beast. The end of innocence, the slaughter of the sow-mother, occurs in Simon's holy place, his sanctuary from the island's frenzy; and, as in Auden's "Musée des Beaux Arts," the butterflies continue their dance amid the bright flow- ers, indifferent to atrocity.

What seems alike is radically different. Ralph, breathless, his face dark from the conch, matches Roger, breathless, with darkened face, stalking his intended victim (18, 68). Simon is as "furtive" entering the forest as Jack, but their purposes are totally dissimilar (61, 53). Simon listens intently to the sounds of the island, with piety and reverence, Jack with a murderous attentiveness, the smell of death in his nostrils: the one hunts truth; the other, pig. The sky is at once the home of the steadfast constellations and another killing field, out of which falls the dead man, answer to the boys' prayer, to topple their precarious society into total dementia. It was precisely this praying for a sign that Christ had forbidden to his disciples, condemning it as the mark of a godless generation. Only once in *Lord of the Flies* is God mentioned, in Ralph's despairing exclamation when he sees the dead signal fire (73). Even with a church choir among them, they seem good modern atheist boys, with religion having either no good influence on their behavior, or, worse still, producing evils in the Lucretian sense—the head choirboy is Beelzebub's high priest. They pray for a sign, not to God, but to the adult world—and the adult world dismayingly complies: you get what you ask for in *Lord of the Flies*.

The island is possessed in two starkly opposed senses: by the lord of dung to whom the tribe pay disgusting homage; and by the spirit of beauty, emanating from great creating nature, the artificer of constellations and butterflies. Man can choose either mode of possession, surrender to the beast or ecstatic acquiescence to the wonder of creation—de Sade's way or Job's. There is no book more brutal or disgusting than *Lord of the Flies*; yet what other work of modern fiction pays such homage to natural beauty? This is why Simon is so crucial to any adequate interpretation of nature in the text, engaging it, as he does, at its most obscene and its most idyllic. He sits in his violated sanctuary, under a clouded sky in tormenting heat, next to a pile of guts, a black blob of buzzing flies, and the pig's head grinning on its stick—nature at its most abhorrently Swiftian (152). Earlier he sits in the same place and imbibes, in a Wordsworthian ecstasy, the beautiful sounds and sights of the island (62). Let nature be your teacher, exhorts Wordsworth; but nature is ambivalent, offering a dual curriculum, and which course you follow depends upon the mind you bring to the tuition. The sermons in stones discovered by Roger are those of Satan: watching the falling coconuts gives him the idea of stoning the littlun. The impulse that Jack gets from a vernal wood is purely destructive: he learns the art of camouflage by studying moths on a tree trunk—it makes him a more effective hunter and killer.

There is no single, unified attitude toward nature in Golding, such as we find in Swift. For Swift, nature is uniformly disgusting: giant cancers, wens, lice, excrement, rats, the monstrous flesh of Brobdingnag, the Yahoo filth of the final voyage—all is revolting. There is no natural beauty in Swift—a character like Simon would be inconceivable in the *Travels*. But in Golding nature wears a Janus face, appearing to the boys in vastly different guises. Some of their initial delight can, doubtless, be explained in terms of the pathetic fallacy. *Esse est percipi*: we project on to the external world our own emotions, making it the mirror of our inner selves. White surf, dark blue sea, dazzling beach—it is the world of the holiday brochures perfected and actualized. Tired and dirty, the boys on their first ascent of the mountain are caught up in the excitement of exploration and easily ignore all discomfort. No doubt, too, there is a touch of conceit, for nature is not only beautiful but apparently man's compliant servant, purveyor of his desires. The things of nature obligingly shape themselves to man's requirements: the fallen tree trunks provide a splendid forum, custom-built for debate; the patch of forest might have been expressly designed for fuel; the act of God, storm or typhoon, that made the miraculous pool, its water warm as a bath, proposes nature as man's architect and engineer (13). It is a world made for us, pandering to our dreams, devoted to our delectation.

The conch is the supreme example of this felicitous adaptation—a thing of nature become a cultural artifact. For Ralph it is simply and uselessly beautiful. It is the practical Piggy, myopically deficient in aesthetic appreciation, who sees its instrumental, its political value: it can be used to summon the others and to regulate discourse when they meet. Piggy not only points this out but shows Ralph how to use the conch. In attributing to Ralph his own common sense, Piggy at once compliments and insults him—because Ralph had *not* seen the use of the conch, but he had seen its beauty, which is denied to Piggy's limited vision. Still, there is no quarrel here between utility and aesthetics: the conch is both *utile et dulce*, useful and beautiful. It therefore symbolizes the first face of nature—a power catering simultaneously to our material welfare and our instinct for delight. *Lord of the Flies* opens as *The Winter's Tale* closes—assuring us that nature is beautiful, harmonious, and devoted to our good.

But, as the boys quickly discover, nature has another, quite different face. Under Piggy's relentless interrogation, Ralph comes to sense a malice in things, a hostility and a threat: "the sun's enmity," "the lagoon attacked them," "invisible arrows," "a blow that they ducked" (15, 67, 63). The boys are on the island because they were attacked, not by the storms of nature, but by the fighter planes of civilization. Gradually, however, it is impressed upon us that there is a nature that is not war's opposite but its continuation. Here Ralph's belt with its snake-clasp may stand as counterpart to the conch. If the conch is a thing of nature transformed beneficently to cultural artifact, the snake-clasp is a human artifact shaped to represent nature at its most insidiously treacherous. Far from being opposites, nature and civilization are assimilated to each other in a conjunction that promises no good to man.

Soon the boys will be terrified of the snake-thing, the beastie, which the littlun claims to have seen. They are right to be afraid when we reflect upon the true identity of the beast. The coming of the choir is crucial to such an understanding. At first Ralph sees what looks like a creature, a serpent, something dark fumbling along the beach. Nearer, the creature becomes an army, uniformed, marching, under command. Serpent and army are nature and civilization at their respectively menacing worst, but in this case they are finally one. "The creature was a party of boys" (20)—but the boys reconstitute themselves as a serpent in the winding procession after the first kill. The story's progress compels us to revise the original revision, to make a reverse identification. Ralph sees a beast that turns out to be a party of boys; at Simon's slaughter the party of boys has become a beast— Ralph's initial "mistake" is, after all, the truth.

Nature is, to some degree, protean to the boys' dispositions. In the night assembly, they become aware of "the evil squeaking" of the trees that goes undetected by day (98)—the nervous, fearful children re-create nature in their own likeness. As darkness falls, Ralph sees his blunder: "We ought to have left all this for daylight" (98). The foolish vote on ghosts would be unthinkable by daylight; in the dark the demons return and the safe world slips away.

But nature also exists in its own right, irrespective of the boys' desires and fears—they have to forget the routines of northern Europe and adapt to the new rhythms of their tropical home. One major misreading of the text is a proposed antithesis between bad nature and good society. It is all too easy to read *Lord of the Flies* as a text that discloses the vicious face of nature beneath the alluring mask, as the paradise turns into a hellhole and Ralph comes to appreciate the lost conveniences of a too easily spurned civilization—toothbrush, washing powder, and all. But the violence of nature is rendered in terms of the destructive society from which the boys have come. From the first description of the black, batlike shape that is the shadow of the human being in sunlight, there is a steady flow of unflattering comparisions of the boys to dogs, blackbirds, pigs—a reduction of the human to the animal (20, 22, 26). The forest fire is likened to a squirrel running from tree to tree, gnawing as it goes, and then, more menacingly, to a jaguar creeping on its belly as it stalks, Roger-like, its prey (48). But soon the trees are exploding like bombs, with the destructiveness of nature linked to high explosives, and the equally insistent allusions to bombs, armies, and warplanes, should dispel any foolish idea that the book is recommending a facile escape into society from anarchic nature. The image of the creepers writhing in the flames combines with the description of the fire's sound as "a drum-roll that seemed to shake the mountain," to bring nature and civilization, snake and drum, together in ominous conjunction (49, 51). Piggy is a victim twice over, of nature and boys alike, a natural victim in every sense, tormented by both asthma and Jack.

The attitude to nature in *Lord of the Flies* is complex, demanding discrimination. There is the attitude of proprietorial delight: *our* island, existing to satisfy *our* desires. There is tonic challenge, the island as something to be overcome, as in the first elated scaling of the mountain. There is disdain and antagonism—Jack slashing contemptuously at the useless green buds, good for nothing. Finally, there is Simon's reverential communion with the island's beauty, aesthetics elevated to mysticism. That this last is the one favored by Golding is surely not in question, since the only real salvation in the text is aesthetic, not moral—or, more precisely, the moral is subsumed in the aesthetic, the world redeemed by beauty, as Dostoyevski's saintly idiot had predicted.

This alone disqualifies Piggy as hero, a position to which some readers are keen to promote him, especially those descended from that erstwhile lover of humanity, pre-Houyhnhnmland Gulliver. It is understandable that those who wish to think well of man should elect Piggy as humanist champion. Angus Wilson may be cited as an admirable representative of this attitude: "We all share . . . an anxiety about modern civilization, but most of us desperately wish that man will in some degree suffice and conquer. We are at our best perhaps where we admit to being humanistic" (Wilson, 247). The modesty of the statement and the vocabulary employed (*anxiety, desperately, admit*) make plain how difficult the enterprise is. Wilson describes Golding as "the nearest to any of us writing in England who is not a humanist," and speculates about his possible Manichaean tendencies: "There are moments when one feels that he thinks that the world is a device of the Devil and that the human race and human species are a mistake. But then one thinks about characters like Piggy (particularly I think of Piggy) and of Simon in *Lord of the Flies*, slaughtered with such enormous compassion and regret, with such deep sense that he wished the world were otherwise. If William Golding is a Manichean, it is with the deepest regret and the greatest wish that he could be more humanistic" (247).

Golding is no Manichaean, as a correct reading of the text makes clear; but basic to such a reading is a recognition of Simon's superiority to his companions, Piggy included. Wilson's preference for Piggy, shown in that revealing parenthesis—his attempt not simply to equate Piggy with Simon, but to rank him higher—produces a distorted exegesis. To regard the boys as somehow equal, the one representing intellect and the other imagination, both qualities being vital for our salvation, is to misconstrue the text. Despite some admirable features, Piggy does not partner, far less rival, Simon as hero—the book, indeed, compels us to choose between them in a far more crucial sense than the choice between Ralph and Jack. Simon is out on his own—for some readers, irritatingly so, since they find him unbelievable or even obscurantist. Golding, counterattacking, retorts that only oversophisticated people will fail to appreciate what Simon represents. This is, of course, arguable and it will continue, quite properly, to be argued. What ought not to be argued is that Golding offers Simon not only as hero but as a disproof of the Manichaean thesis that Beelzebub rules the material world. Those who prefer Piggy as the most practical option available to us must be allowed their opinion, but only on condition that they do not foist it onto Golding; if Piggy is the humanists' choice, Simon is Golding's.

Piggy and Simon are at once the most original creations in the book and the representatives of its deepest and innermost dialectic. In contrasting the flawed decency and limited common sense of the one with the vatic insight and mystic intuition of the other, we disclose the unique meaning of *Lord of the Flies*, especially in its final, creative divergence from the tradition of the dark epiphany.

Piggy is a much more complex character than the oversimplified interpretations so regularly adduced allow. The very fact that his unremitting common sense chimes in so well with Ballantyne's ethos might give us pause before hailing him as hero—*The Coral Island* is just as scathing as Piggy about the possibility of ghosts, and for much the same reason. This common sense is evident from the start as he organizes the meeting and tries to make a list of everyone present—the attendance register transplanted to the jungle. Significantly, Piggy's action foreshadows the first question put by the rescuing officer; he wants to know how many boys there are and is both disappointed and a little shocked to hear that English boys in particular have not made even this elementary calculation. Piggy might legitimately claim to be absolved from blame.

Yet he is a doubtful hero who, no sooner met, has to rush away from us in a bout of diarrhea; in addition, he wears spectacles, suffers from asthma, is fat through eating too many sweets in his auntie's shop, can't swim or run, and—most important of all—speaks abysmal English, which stamps him as unmistakably working-class. He is doubly out of place—what, one wonders, was he doing on the plane with boys so clearly his social superiors? Neither Ralph nor Jack would have met Piggy back in England save as their employee, for while they are so obviously, in their respective ways, officer material, he is just as clearly born to remain an underling all his days.

Yet it is Piggy who has a monopoly on common sense and practical intelligence. Jack, instinctively recognizing an inferior and a target of abuse, orders him to be quiet, yet no one else talks such consistent good sense. Ironically, in the increasingly hysterical atmosphere, his common sense turns out to be as much of a handicap as his bad eyesight. Nowhere is Orwell's description of England as a family with the wrong members in control so visibly demonstrated as in the way the leadership contest becomes a fight between Ralph and Jack, with Piggy not even considered, far less chosen. Yet who better to elect, given that clear thinking, with a view to maximizing the chances of rescue, is the main priority? Jack knows that he should be leader and tells the others why: he can sing C-sharp. The sheer irrelevance of this is not meant to make us laugh but shiver: the führer's lust for power needs no justification other than his own irrational conviction of merit. Yet the choice of Ralph, as Golding makes plain, is just as irrational: Ralph becomes leader because he looks like one—he gets the job on appearance and not ability. His very stillness is charismatic: he only has to sit and look the part.

Piggy lacks the looks but has the know-how. The trouble is that he knows but cannot do, and so is relegated, in accordance with Shaw's dictum, to being at best a teacher. He cannot blow the conch himself— the asthma again—but he sees its practical possibilities and shows Ralph how to use it. He never advances his own claims to leadership— though, significantly, his is the last hand, Jack's apart, to be grudgingly raised when Ralph is elected. Thereafter, however, he is Ralph's loyal adviser and policy maker. *Lord of the Flies* does not, like *The Admirable Crichton*, depict the rise of a meritocracy, when, following the social upheaval of shipwreck, the supremely efficient butler takes over as leader of the feckless aristocrats, to relapse into subordination only when the party is rescued and taken back to the home counties from the jungle. Ralph and Jack are leaders in the jungle as they would be in England. Barrie's aristocrats, recognizing the demands of reality, resign themselves to accepting a social inferior as their natural leader; Golding's boys would hoot at the idea of taking orders from Piggy.

What is interesting is the skillful way in which Golding employs the prejudices of the English class system to support his allegorical intention. The allegory requires that the boys should undervalue, ignore, even despise common sense. How shrewd, in that case, to embody it in a fat, bespectacled, unathletic working-class boy who is the natural target of middle-class contempt. The language barrier is the crucial thing. Crichton, after all, speaks impeccable English, but what gentleman could ever bring himself to take orders from someone who speaks like Piggy? Piggy can aspire, at most, to advise, and he is, to begin with, the best adviser that Ralph could have. We must not, of course, push the allegory to the absurd extreme of saying that the working class has all the common sense, but we are entitled—even obliged—to point out that the task set common sense in the book becomes infinitely more difficult by making its personification a work-ing-class boy among upper-class companions.

Although not primarily interested in class, Golding is far from ignorant about it. The allegorical insistence throughout that men prefer passion to practicality and glamour to common sense is reinforced by the realism of social antipathy. Piggy, trained to know his place, does not protest, far less rebel, against this. From the moment Jack appears, common sense takes a backseat, and the reason is unarguably con-nected with the English class system. Piggy at once stops taking names for his list: "He was intimidated by this uniformed superiority and the offhand authority in Merridew's voice. He shrank to the other side of Ralph and busied himself with his glasses" (22). Piggy knows he is inferior, just as Ralph and Jack take their superiority for granted.

It is this sense of inferiority that makes him deliver himself into the hands of his class enemies right from the start, when he foolishly tells Ralph his derisory nickname and even more foolishly asks him to keep it a secret. It is perhaps unfair to say that Ralph betrays him, since betrayal implies a confidence solicited and a promise broken, and Ralph does neither; but at the first opportunity Ralph blurts out Piggy's secret to the whole world. Even Ralph, so straight and decent, is not above meanness; his tears for Piggy at the close are an act of contrition for all the insults and injuries, climaxing in murder, which the boys from the start inflict upon their inferior companion. In Ralph, at least, class contempt is thoroughly overcome, as he weeps for the true, wise friend who came to him originally in such an unprepossessing guise.

That Piggy does to some extent bring his troubles upon himself leaves unchallenged his claim to be *the* sensible person on the island. He himself never makes this claim because he only partially realizes it. Among his limitations is a tendency to credit others with his own good sense. He keeps attributing to Ralph his own practical insights when it is plain that Ralph is still fumbling around in the dark. He rebukes the other boys for distracting Ralph from what he was about to say and then puts the words into his bemused leader's mouth. There is nothing devious or disingenuous in this. Piggy shares Ballantyne's confidence that common sense can master any problem, and he believes

110

that most people, given the chance, are as sensible as himself. When, after Ralph's first speech—Piggy admires it as a model of succinct good sense—the other boys, led by Jack, run off in disorganized excitement to light the signal fire, Ralph and Piggy are left alone with the conch; then Ralph, too, scrambles after "the errant assembly," leaving disgusted common sense on its own. All Piggy can do is toil breathlessly after them while venting his indignation in the worst reproof he can muster: "Acting like a crowd of kids!" (42).

But that's what they are. The book shows that you get an old head on young shoulders only when the shoulders are those of a podgy, unhealthy, humiliated boy. "A youth who is invariably reasonable does not inspire much confidence and isn't worth much": we may accept Dostoyevsky's defense of his hero, Alyosha (*Karamazov*, 397), without feeling obliged to use it as a condemnation of Piggy. Nevertheless, there is a sense in which Piggy is too humdrum to be heeded. Ironically, the adult the boys desperately need is among them, but so impenetrably disguised as not to be recognized, let alone obeyed. Piggy's continual annoyance and much less justified continual surprise at the folly of his companions might have led him to suspect that his own common sense was not so widely distributed as he imagined, yet right up to his destruction he goes on believing in the power of reason to tame the beast. His most fervent exhortation to the others is to stop being kids and instead to think and act like adults; therein, he believes, lies salvation. One of the book's cruelest ironies is that the boys finally take his advice: they act like adults and kill him.

Yet in this ambivalent book where everything is double, it is fitting that Piggy's handicaps, most notably his asthma, should also be compensations. Sickness brings its own insights; Simon, as has been noted, is the supreme exemplification of this psychological truth. Long before anyone else, Piggy senses the menace of Jack and the element of self-interest in the intuition makes it no less valid. Allegorically, it represents the fact that reason and common sense are the prey of fanaticism. Piggy is stricken when Ralph talks despairingly of surrendering to Jack: 'If you give up,' said Piggy in an appalled whisper, 'what'ud happen to me? . . . He hates me. I dunno why' (102). On the naturalistic level this is perfectly credible—a little boy, with every cause to be frightened of a bully, expresses his own personal fears—but allegorically we note the impotence of common sense to check the progress of demented totalitarianism: when Jack is frustrated, his eyes are described as bolting, blazing, or mad.

Orwell, in what was almost a kind of parricide, attacked H. G. Wells for complacently dismissing Hitler as a presumptuous nonentity doomed to defeat because he was the enemy of reason (Orwell, *Essays*, 2:170–71). In *Nineteen Eighty-four* Winston Smith has all the reason on his side, but his enemy, O'Brien, has all the power. Golding reenacts the same conflict in a children's playground, emptied of teachers, to impart the same lesson. Piggy perceptively associates his fear of Jack with his sickness: "You kid yourself he's all right really, an' then when you see him again it's like asthma an' you can't breathe" (102). When Ralph tries to pooh-pooh this as exaggeration, Piggy confides the source of his superior insight: "I been in bed so much I done some thinking. I know about people. I know about me. And him" (102). If the grammar is faulty, the psychology is sound: Piggy does know about Jack, before anyone else does, and his knowledge springs from the kind of boy he is. The ailment that has stopped him from being an athlete has encouraged him to be a thinker, though (and the qualification is crucial) a thinker of a limited kind.

There is certainly much to admire in Piggy. His liberal-democratic outlook and sense of fair play lead him to the honorable idea that everyone, however lowly, has a right to speak—even a littlun who wants the conch must be given it. Again, Jack is the adversary. "We don't need the conch any more. We know who ought to say things" (111). This leads straight to an Asiatic-style court where only the tyrant's voice is heard because all dissenters have been put to death; Piggy supports a polyphonic society, Jack a society of mutes, since men need only ears to hear the master's dictates.

Piggy, too, is the first to recognize that life entails making certain choices and establishing certain priorities. Ralph, by contrast, tells the boys what mankind has always wished to hear: that there is no troublesome competition among our desires, that the world will complaisantly minister to all our wishes, that fun and rescue fit easily into one package. (*Fun* is a word to watch in *Lord of the Flies*, for on the three important occasions when it is used—by Ralph, by Beelzebub in his warning to Simon, and by the rescuing officer—it sets alarm bells ringing [41, 159, 221].

It is the practical Piggy who jarringly introduces the reality principle into the dream of pleasure: "How can you expect to be rescued if you don't put first things first and act proper?" (50). The grammatical solecism should not obscure the moral wisdom. Life is not the Hilton, but a series of harsh choices and necessary sacrifices; if you are lucky, you will get what you deserve but there will be no windfalls. Piggy stands for the Judeo-Christian conditional promise upon which our civilization once rested: you can either eat the apple or stay in Eden— not both; you shall reach the Promised Land, but only after the discipline of an arduous journey through the wilderness. Piggy introduces the unpleasant idea of incompatible desires: do you want fun or rescue? If rescue is the first priority, then fun must come a poor second. If we are serious about rescue, that means work, and work is what we would prefer someone else to do: lighting and maintaining fires, building shelters, and all the other tedious chores that the little folk in fairy tales perform for a bowl of milk. Civilization, says Freud, is based upon the renunciation of instinctual gratification, and Piggy is, so it seems, the only Freudian on the island.[9] *Lord of the Flies* depicts the disintegration of a society whose members play rather than work.

Self-denial is the infallible litmus test. When Jack goes hunting, he is clearly doing something that is both demanding and dangerous—instinctual gratification is not necessarily immersion in sybaritic hedonism. The point is that Jack is doing what he wants, not what he ought; he relishes the danger of the chase and the excitement of the kill. Piggy does not criticize Jack for doing what is easy, but for putting his own pleasure above the common good. Stalking pigs is thrilling, tending a fire dull, so Jack opts for Yahoo excitement in preference to Houyhnhnm tedium—this makes him the foe of Piggy and civilization alike. The trouble is that Jack is more representative than Piggy, and his outlook prevails, even though not all of the defaulters are pursuing pigs with the indefatigable hunter—most have plumped for Tahiti, for fruit, sunbathing and swimming. At assemblies they all vote dutifully for the laudable resolutions because people love to talk, but they do not love to work: "We decide things. But they don't get done . . . [86] people don't help much" (59). And so the huts, vital to civilized survival, are either unbuilt or ramshackle. It is hard to be civilized, deleteriously easy to be savage. Work is irksome: in terms of this Kantian definition, Jack would be a layabout even if he chased pigs from dawn to dusk.

We must, accordingly, be careful not to be too harsh on Piggy for being such a bore; even Ralph, despite their growing friendship, sees his failing: "his fat, his ass-mar, and his matter-of-fact ideas were dull" (70). Piggy *is* depressingly literalist, totally lacking in a sense of humor, taking everything so seriously—how can he write to his auntie, he answers the sarcastic Ralph, when there isn't a postman to collect his letter? (182–83). His complete incapacity for irony—which is a kind of double-talk—is an ominous indication of his disastrously one-eyed view of things. His proposal to make a sundial (presumably to know when it is teatime) provokes the increasingly exasperated Ralph to suggest making a jet plane as well; Piggy, having duly considered this, solemnly replies that they lack the necessary materials (70). Simon's irrational assurance that Ralph will one day return home is far less infuriating than Piggy's obtuse and obsolete logic—there is no more teatime on the island. The world of the prophet may or may not be a delusion; the world of the sweetshop is unquestionably an irrelevance. Simon may save us, Piggy cannot.

Nevertheless, Piggy is decent, and the book insists upon the superiority of dull decency to the heady intoxication of evil, even if it also exposes the sad insufficiency of the former. The Yahoos, in any case, pay a heavy price for all that life they are supposed to possess. The two worlds are dramatically contrasted when Jack, fresh from his first, elated kill, the bloodied knife in his hand, confronts Ralph, fuming because the chance of rescue has been lost: "the brilliant world of hunting, tactics, fierce exhilaration, skill" versus the antithetical world of "longing and baffled common-sense" (77). We *must* choose between pigs and huts, hunters and builders, fun and rescue. If Piggy is dull, he is also right.

Only to a certain degree, however, because his intelligence is seriously limited. The sole, damaging occasion when he agrees with Jack is to deny the beast's existence. Jack initially insists, with fine positivist arrogance, that there is no beast—he has hunted all over the island and "if there were a beast I'd have seen it" (91). Piggy ominously joins his enemy, the pig-killer, in dismissing the idea of a beast—"of course there isn't nothing to be afraid of in the forest"—though he approaches Simon's intuition in stating that "there isn't no fear . . . unless we get frightened of people" (92). Simon, however, means that fear, like charity, should begin at home—the beast is within each of us. Piggy fears only the other—Jack is the beast, and if only he had died in the crash, all would be well. That, clearly, is not what Golding believes.

Piggy's chief handicap is his unfounded trust in a rational universe administered by rational man: "Life is scientific, that's what it is"; "We know what goes on and if there's something wrong, there's someone to put it right" (92, 91). Everything comes right in the end: this is the root fallacy of the liberal mind that Orwell identified and pilloried in *Nineteen Eighty-four*. Piggy has teamed up with the complacent optimists he formerly rebuked.

It is Simon, a character not to be found, however faintly, in Ballantyne's story, whom Golding uses to highlight Piggy's shortcomings. Piggy is merely the theoretician of hard work, but "Simon helps"—helps Ralph to build the huts, serves the littluns fruit from the high trees, goes to Piggy's assistance when his glasses are broken in the scuffle with Jack (59, 61, 78). Golding's paradox is that the antisocial recluse, going away from his fellows to commune with nature, is also the most socially committed of all the boys on the island, forever available when needed, instantaneously willing, as in the journey alone through the dark forest to rejoin Piggy, to perform the tasks from which everyone else shrinks. Simon is the personification of doubleness in the text, not simply *seeing* it, but, more important still, *being* it. Piggy's help, by contrast, is invariably a verbal affair; he can tell people the right kind of wood to gather for the fire—but don't ask him to gather it. Even allowing for the asthma, one must conclude that he is lazy, his Freudian commitment to work more apparent than real.

The distance separating Piggy from Simon—it is totally misleading to represent them as allies somehow unfortunately estranged—is indicated in Piggy's shocked incomprehension at Simon's tentative suggestion that perhaps there *is* a beast and that "maybe it's only us." Piggy indignantly rejects this as "nuts!" (97). Such mystical speculations not only are beyond his limitedly sensible mind, but strike him as a shamefully foolish betrayal of the humanist tradition for which he stands. He neither can nor will assist Simon in the latter's inarticulate effort to express man's essential illness. For Piggy man is *not* ill—he just has a foolish but corrigible habit of following Jack when he should be taking Piggy's sensible advice. Piggy is still handing out this sensible advice when the boulder shatters him to pieces. Simon's stumbling attempt to explain the beast provokes general derision, which Piggy orchestrates—but, as the book shows, it is the mystic who is right and the mockers who are wrong.

Ralph reveals a similar incapacity for Simon's insight and reproaches him for voicing such a distressing thought: "Why couldn't you say there wasn't a beast?" (102). Say what we want to hear or nothing at all. But Piggy characteristically supplies the rationale for dismissing Simon as witless. There is no beast for the same reason that there are no ghosts, "'cos things wouldn't make sense. Houses an' streets, an'—TV—they wouldn't work" (101). Piggy will pay for this empty faith with his life, but, even as he speaks, the argument is sorrily unconvincing. Europe has been destroyed in nuclear war and its exiled sons, led by Jack, chant and dance like savages while Piggy makes his pitiful profession of faith: *credo quia impossible est* (I believe because it is impossible).

Ralph and Piggy fail to see that, in silencing Simon, they are in effect surrendering to Jack. The book traces three routes for mankind: Piggy's common sense, Jack's demonism, and Simon's mysticism. But common sense is intimidated by demonism—Piggy is terrified in Jack's presence. The paradox is that the mystic way, which strikes Piggy as outrageous mumbo jumbo, is the truly practical solution. Simon is the real skeptic because he cannot believe the twins' story of a beast with claws that sat on a mountaintop, left no tracks, and yet was not fast enough to catch Samneric (113). It is Simon who proves that if you don't stand for something, you'll fall for anything. This same practical sense is made evident when the boys huddle in crazed despair after the apparent confirmation of the twins' story. Ralph has just gloomily announced that there is nothing to be done when Simon reaches for the conch. Ralph's irritation is plain: "Simon? What is it this time?" (141). Bad enough to be leader in such a predicament without having to listen to a crackpot, but what Simon says takes the all-time gold medal for sheer looniness: "I think we ought to climb the mountain" (142). Piggy receives this suggestion with open-mouthed incomprehension and no one even bothers to answer the cretin when he asks, "What else is there to do?" (142). Piggy's solution—to cede the mountain to the beast and shift the signal fire to a safer place—is applauded by the boys as a stroke of intellectual audacity. Yet Simon's is the truly intrepid invitation in every sense of the word—intellectually, morally, and psychologically—for it *is* the only thing to do: we must outstare Medusa, face and outface what we fear, or be afraid forever. Piggy will tell you how to hide from fear, Simon how to vanquish it. Either the beast rules or we do: surrendering the mountain is admitting that the contest is over: one might as well go the whole way and join Jack in devil-worship, in full propitiation of the demon.

Simon knows how to deal with the beast because he knows who it is: "However Simon thought of the beast, there rose before his inward sight the picture of a human at once heroic and sick" (113). Piggy is incapable of such an intuition. In his secret place among the leaves Simon's recognition of the beast enables him to solve the problem that leaves the others in baffled anguish. While he is unlocking the secret, Ralph is asking why things have gone so terribly wrong and making one more vain appeal to common sense. Surely if a doctor told the boys to take medicine or die, they would do the sensible thing? Why, then, can't they see the equal importance of the signal fire? Why do you have to beg people to save themselves? The mystery tortures him without respite: "Just an ordinary fire. You'd think we could do that, wouldn't you? Just a smoke signal so we can be rescued. Are we savages or what?" (188). Ralph appeals piteously to Piggy ("What's wrong? . . . what makes things break up like they do?") but Piggy's only answer is to blame Jack (154). This is true only in the allegorical sense, but Piggy, not knowing that he, Jack, and the others are characters in an allegory, blames Jack as an individual, and this is hopelessly inadequate. Jack is to blame only in the sense that he lives in all of us, that we are all guilty because mankind is sick.

Simon is the one exception to this general condemnation. The epileptic is the one spiritually sound person on the island, and, further paradox, it is his sickness that helps to make him a saint. Simon is not interested in leadership or any other form of competitive self-assertion; the nature of reality, not the promotion of the self, is his preoccupation. He is one of the meek, the poor in spirit, who are promised the kingdom of heaven, not the plaudits and rewards of earthly assemblies. His very debility is to be seen as a mark of the divine at work in him. While Ralph and Piggy wrestle in vain with the *mysterium iniquitatis*, Simon is shut up in audience with the Lord of the Flies. Piggy, the visible son of Polyphemus, is only partially right: There *is* nothing to fear in the forest, but that is because the beast is within man; the only forest to fear is the heart of darkness. "Fancy thinking the Beast was something you could hunt and kill! . . . You knew, didn't you? I'm part of you? Close, close, close! I'm the reason why it's no go? Why things are what they are?" (158). Beelzebub invites Simon to join him in deriding the stupidity of the other boys—what further proof of Simon's superior insight is required when the evil one himself acknowledges it?

From the first men in *The Inheritors* to the atomic killers of today the same root delusion persists: evil is external, the act of the other; we, innocent and threatened, will pursue and destroy it, and only thus will the world be cleansed. Beelzebub warns the boy who has broken the secret not to interfere with the "fun" about to take place or else "we shall do you"; significantly, "we" includes Piggy and Ralph as well as Jack and Roger (159); Simon is the single immaculate conception in Golding's fable. When he ignores the threat and tries to bring the good news to the other boys, Beelzebub's promise is hideously fulfilled.

We touch here the most startling paradox of a paradoxical book: Simon's good news is that *we* are sick, not the world. Evil does not sit alien and invincible on a mountain, mocking our futile hope of rescue; evil is within and can be mastered. Christ had likewise insisted that only an inner pollution can kill the soul, and with Simon the Christian symbolism of the text becomes unmistakable. His dying words about a dead man on a hill evoke an image of Calvary, and his own death is clearly intended as a recapitulation of that ancient sacrifice—nothing changes in the way men treat their redeemers.

Simon is the most original and contentious creation in *Lord of the Flies*, the cause of the most serious rift among the critics, the rock indeed upon which much opinion founders. Some find him thoroughly unconvincing, his shoulders far too slight to sustain the weight of symbolic import laid upon them: would a little boy possess such mystic insight? His actions, it is alleged, are motivated not by the dramatic situation but by the symbolical requirements of the story—Golding is so intent on his moral message that he does not hesitate to make the youngsters, especially Simon, dance to his tune (Johnston, 11; Townsend, 154–56). The scene between Simon and the beast is cited as a particularly flagrant instance of this authorial choreography.

"In writing of this kind all depends upon the author's mythopoeic power to transcend the programme" (Kermode, *Puzzles*, 205). The words are a salutary reminder that we are reading a work of art, not a historical document. If Golding can persuade us to accept one little boy as the prince of hell, Beelzebub's acolyte, there seems no good reason to jib when he proposes a second little boy as the son of God. It all depends not on any a priori considerations of credibility, but on whether it works within the text. On this criterion, only those resolved in advance to withhold approval will deny Golding's achievement.

What Simon stands for is textually manifest, and Golding has confirmed this in discussing his book. Simon is saint, mystic, clairvoyant, a proof for the illiterate that God exists: the son must have a father—a person like Simon necessarily implies a good god. But intention is one thing, achievement another: how successful is Golding in his presentation of Simon? The question is the more crucial in that it determines how we read *Lord of the Flies*; to reject Simon as incredible and unconvincing is to pronounce the book wholly pessimistic, since it means, in effect, relinquishing the material world to the Lord of the Flies. For Jack, nature is a haunted and frantic affair, a matter of stalking and blood; following his brief holiday euphoria, Ralph's experience of nature is one of disillusion and despair.

Turning from his guilty companions, the stealthy excreters, Ralph looks at the sea and shudders, seeing for the first time, without the screen of the lagoon, the vast swell of the ocean, a "stupendous creature," a "sleeping leviathan" (115). There are two islands with totally different faces. On the protected side, one can dream of rescue amid the mirages: here is deceptive nature, the cheat castigated so fiercely by Spenser and Bunyan. On the exposed side, there is brutal truth— the demoralizing immensity of ocean. This is not the cute wildness of Dartmoor ponies or the tranquil harmony of Simon's night watch, not the gift assigned to man by Genesis, but the nature invoked by God to quell Job's puny questioning, the nature that terrified Pascal with the silence of its infinite spaces, the nature of Shelley's Ozymandias consigning man's life and all its silly striving to futility and oblivion.

How can one look on this and still dream of rescue or even believe that man is worth rescuing? How can the human being matter in this indifferent vastness? "Soon, in a matter of centuries . . ." (115)— already man's span has been trivialized by geological time. To this is added a spatial put-down, the vast Pacific contributing to man's cosmic humiliation, time and space combining to reduce man to his exiguous place in the scheme of things. It is at this moment of total intimidation that Simon prophesies rescue for Ralph—though, significantly, not for himself—and the text finally vindicates him: believe and you shall be saved. Simon's intervention, his challenge to nature's apparent indifference, compels the reader to ponder the source of his assurance.

There are only two possibilities: either he is a simpleton, dreamily imbecilic, or he is a seer with access to secret knowledge denied the other boys. Can it be seriously questioned which of these judgments the text sustains? That nature will respond to us in kind, presenting a murderous face to the murderer, a face of despair to the desponder, a serene countenance to the mystic, is a truth abundantly confirmed in this text. Jack, slashing in rage at the useless buds, avidly scanning the ground for pig droppings, gets the nature (and the God) he deserves. Simon makes a contemplative paradise of the same island. Blessed are the pure in heart for they shall see God. Simon sees the holiness of creation from his forest-retreat. The darkness that terrifies the others pours down upon him like a benediction. The night world seems like the bottom of the sea, but a life-giving sea, the sea of Ariel's song in *The Tempest*. There are echoes of *The Tempest* throughout *Lord of the Flies*: a shipwreck, transactions with evil, a final ambiguous rescue. "Holding his breath he cocked a critical ear at the sounds of the island" (62). As Simon listens in love, the lines of *The Tempest* are pertinent: "Be not afeared; the air is full of noises,

Sounds, and sweet airs, that give delight and hurt not."[10]

Simon's oneness with nature is shown in the match between the sound of the sea and the susurration of his blood. The candle-buds, despised by Jack, open their flowers to "the light that pricked down from the first stars. Their scent spilled out into the air and took possession of the island" (62). So must unfallen Adam have experienced the first night of creation. This "possessed" island does not belong to Beelzebub; the demons of Gadarea have no residence here. The whole passage is a great tone poem, a hymn to creation and a testimony to the ultimate rightness of existence, inconceivable in *Gulliver's Travels* or *Robinson Crusoe*. The great mystics and poets are the context that the passage demands—it is not to be comprehended within the categories of Augustan reason or nineteenth-century realism. This is

Simon's natural setting, associated as he is throughout with stillness and harmony. Nature gives him in death no more than his due, a truth emphasized the more when we contrast his passage from life with the brutal exit of Piggy.

Nowhere is the misguided attempt to equate Piggy with Simon in a kind of dual heroism more clearly discredited than in their startlingly different deaths, the one richly religious, the other starkly secular—to appreciate this is to identify the true hero, the book's only redeemer. The change in tone and perspective is remarkable as we pass from the horror of Simon's murder, from the storm's rage and the ritual's frenzy, to the absolution of cleansing, healing nature. The diminuendo is signaled by the typographical device of the dropped line, visibly marking the shift from bloodlust to benediction (169). It is almost as though, in the atmosphere of uncontaminated serenity that follows, nature were striving to atone for the previous wickedness: "The incredible lamps of stars . . . the drop and trickle of water . . . the air was cool, moist, and clear"; finally, with wonderful impact, "presently even the sound of the water was still" (169). In this soundless world of pure beauty, even the sound of the tide's advance must be taken on trust: "it accepted . . . with an inaudible syllable and moved on" (169). Never was a godlike narrator more appropriate than to this godlike scene. The edge of the lagoon is transformed into a streak of phosphorescence. Everything is seen, nothing heard. This is a pictorial art as evocative as anything in Spenser or Tennyson—here Golding is to be ranked with the poets rather than the novelists: "The great wave of the tide flowed. The clear water mirrored the clear sky and the bright angular constellations" (169). Whenever Golding wishes to reassure, he turns to a nature—ocean, sky, stars—beyond human contamination; "look you, the stars shine still."[11] How could such a universe belong to Beelzebub or its depicter be described as Manichaean? This is Prince Myshkin's salvation through beauty, the world become a sacrament, the outward sign of an abiding inner grace. That only Simon merits so lovely a quietus is incontestable proof of his unique importance to the text.

In this triumph over hideous death is the book's sole salvation. Simon's lovingly adorned, meticulously tended corpse is reverently received by an ocean unrecognizable from the one that appalled Ralph, full of life and beauty. "The advancing clearness" is "full of strange, moonbeam-bodied creatures with fiery eyes"; the pebbles are "covered with a coat of pearls"; "the rain-pitted sand" (with blood stains from the broken body) is smoothed over with a layer of silver (169). Nature brings to the dead child gifts surpassing those that the Magi brought to the living one. There is now no indignity or humiliation, no mockery by nature as with the poor corpse of the dead parachutist—nature is now the most reverent of ministrants, the most solicitous of mourners. Ariel's song of metamorphosis in *The Tempest* or the flights of angels taking Hamlet to his rest: such is the context in which Simon's passage to eternity is to be understood. "Truly this was the son of God": the words of the awed centurion under the black sky that both mourned and resented the death of Christ—this or something akin should be our reaction as nature witnesses in similar fashion the death of another boy. "The creatures made a moving patch of light as they gathered at the edge" (169): it is a measure of Golding's artistic control that he can risk the pun at so critical a moment, for it is, indeed, the most moving passage in the book. All disagreeables are evaporated, in Keats's phrase, as atrocity is alchemized into art.

As in *The Winter's Tale*, there is a union of art and nature to produce the sense of a world ransomed. Simon's coarse hair is dressed with brightness, the line of his cheek is silvered, the turn of his shoulder becomes sculpted marble. In death Simon *becomes* a new creation, a work of art, as nature turns into the most attentive of artist-morticians —painter, sculptor, engraver—to confer what the artist has always claimed to be able to confer: immortality upon otherwise condemned flesh. Simon consoles the abject Ralph, assuring him that while there's life there's hope; it is mere justice that for himself there should be beauty in death. The "attendant creatures" that form his cortège are servers like himself, not self-servers like Jack and Roger—what could be fairer than that Simon, so caring for others in life, should himself be so lovingly cared for in death? The universe is, despite the horror, ultimately just and righteous. "Softly, surrounded by a fringe of bright, inquisitive creatures, itself a silver shape beneath the steadfast constellations, Simon's bright body moved out towards the open sea" (170). This beautiful end to a vile beginning invokes the world of the mystics, especially the serene assurance of Dame Julian of Norwich: "Sin is behovely but all shall be well and all shall be well and all manner of things shall be well" (Norwich, 57).

To repeat: either Simon is imbecile or he has a "supernatural" insight into reality denied the other boys. The novel forbids the first alternative. Simon awkwardly confounds all simplistic readings, as, for example, the argument that the novel is an "Augustinian" or "tory" book, upholding law and order against anarchic misrule and licentious freedom. All of the boys, so it is argued, removed from the pinfold of civilization, inevitably regress to savagery. But this is untrue of Simon; in the jungle he becomes prophet and redeemer, and it would be absurd to argue that he inherits these roles as a result of a sound education in the home counties. The island brings him out as much as it does Roger: if it is to be blamed for the second "education," it should, in fairness, be praised for the first. Simon is not one up for civilization in its neverending quarrel with nature—if anything, the beautiful resumption of his body by the ocean might lend support to nature's advocates.

But it is misleading to use Simon as a counter in the culture-nature wrangle, since he transcends both to become in every sense, artistic and Pauline, a new creation. Why did Golding create him and why is his hideous death followed by so moving a requiescat, in stark contrast to the brutal disposal of the dead Piggy? Only the determinedly deaf will contrive to miss the religious reverberations of the passage describing the dead boy's transfiguration—the gentle escort of the body to the sea is as close to a resurrection as so secular a form as the novel dare come. More than a simple sea change is involved: this new beauty is clearly the servant of some greater purpose, positing an alternative world opposed to the nightmare world of blood and taboo, a world, in Hopkins's words, charged with the glory of God. The passage provides a sacramental guarantee that creation is not just some haphazard collision of atoms but the product of an organizing power, a power which promises, not simply rest, but resurrection to those who sacrifice themselves for its sake. Rhythm and imagery make it impossible to believe that Simon's death is merely another bloody atrocity, pointless and inane, clinching proof in this dark book that life is a tale told by an idiot. The sense of peace informing the passage is not simply that which Macbeth envies in Duncan. Simon *is* out of the madness, he *is* at rest—after the fever of the island he sleeps well—but not just in the negative sense of Macbeth's longing; the peace that concludes Simon's sacrifice is much more akin to the promise of the beatitude: blessed are the pure in heart for they shall see God. Simon is now completely at one with whatever strong, beautiful power it is that sustains creation, the power that will continue to maintain "the steadfast constellations" when all the hagridden acolytes of Beelzebub have followed Macbeth to vacuous death. It is an arresting peripeteia: the dark epiphany is pierced by a shaft of light from that other epiphany, promising salvation and for once Dame Julian's promise is echoed in the century of revocation.

Simon in death is vindicated: there is no rescue for those who will not climb the mountain. This represents a failure far more catastrophic for Piggy than for Jack. Jack's irrationalism thrives on lies, but Piggy's practical intelligence must respect truth or it is good for nothing. Piggy starts off shortsighted, becomes one-eyed, and, finally, his glasses stolen, is completely blind: in terms of the allegory, it is a depressing career for common sense. His reverence for the conch is at once exemplary and absurd, touching and ludicrous—it raises questions as to whether men can live by their own consciously created myths; the conch is, after all, just a thing that they fished out of the water, its only sanctity being what they decide to grant it. Can a myth, once seen through, continue to be effective? As with his common sense, Piggy tends to attribute his own values to everyone else. Despite Jack's unconcealed contempt for the conch from the start, Piggy foolishly believes that the purpose of Jack's raid was to seize the conch, not the glasses. To the end he clings to the delusion of legitimacy, as obsolete as teatime. The blind boy demands, with heroic idiocy, to be led by his friends to the evil fortress where he will confront the tyrant with "the one thing he hasn't got": the precious conch (189). Decency will put power to shame; right will challenge might and will prevail. This passionate readiness to carry his talisman against all the odds is at once a tribute to his commitment and a mark of his folly, guaranteeing destruction. The savages giggle when Ralph accuses their chief of not "playing the game"—as though, in stealing Piggy's glasses, Jack has merely broken some schoolboy code instead of becoming the thief of fire.

Piggy is still trying to reason in bedlam: "Which is better—to be a pack of painted niggers like you are, or to be sensible like Ralph is?" (199). The question, as misplaced as it is sensible, falls on derisory ears. Piggy continues to treat the savages like a bunch of scatterbrained kids, implying that if they behaved like adults, all would be well. It is understandable that he should blame the collapse on the absence of adults, but the text disallows so simplistic an attribution. The boys may be forgiven for craving "the majesty of adult life"; adults know better (103). What the boys fail to see, with Piggy the most egregious offender, is that children are but men of smaller growth; the boys would not be on the island at all but for the far more terrible quarrels of their childish fathers. The boys are their fathers' sons—by what miracle can they transcend their begetting? When Roger, looking down on the bag of fat, releases, "with a sense of delirious abandonment," the great rock that kills the advocate of common sense, he is not acting like a kid but like the depraved adults who have plunged the world into nuclear war in the first place (200). Conch and common sense are shattered together and there is nothing healing or transfiguring about this death.

So glaring is the difference between the two deaths that some might feel provoked to protest the injustice of Piggy's treatment. Antigone, defying Creon, declares that "death longs for the same rites for all."[12] Not if we are to judge by *Lord of the Flies*. All the poetic resources of language, so cunningly mustered for Simon's obsequies, are brutally eschewed in the curt description of Piggy's death. Golding manifestly does not want poetry, but the starkest of prose, for Piggy's demise. Within four lines his life ends and his corpse is gone: "Piggy's arms and legs twitched a bit, like a pig's after it has been killed. Then the sea breathed again in a low slow sigh, the water boiled white and pink over the rocks and when it went, sucking back again, the body of Piggy was gone" (200). There is not even a grunt as the boiling water—a very different sea from that which had done Simon such reverence—receives Piggy like so much pork. The terseness borders on cruelty. It is the language of prose; the sigh of the sea is a minimal concession to poetry, since the preceding simile presents Piggy as animal, the bag of fat that Roger finds irresistible.

Simon's obsequies are those of hero, saint, martyr: an essentially religious affair. Piggy's death is that of an animal, an abattoir slaughter, performed with dispatch, barren of ritual and respect: he falls forty feet, lands on his back, and "his head opened and stuff came out and turned red"—the brains that Ralph had come to envy (200). There is here no slow, dignified, funeral procession to the sea; instead, the sea behaves toward Piggy's body like some fairground cardsharp in a kind of now-you-see-it, now-you-don't performance. Surely, we protest, Piggy deserves better than this? But nature will not take instructions from us—she administers the viaticum she thinks fit. Simon, the beloved son, is transfigured, but Piggy, his animal associations notwithstanding, has no relation to nature—he is purely a product of society, and of society at a fairly vulgar level: not the life of culture or intellect, but of television and teatime, solecisms and sweets. As you live, so shall you die: the pitiless dismissal of Piggy is enough in itself to demolish any pretensions to a copartnership in heroism, let alone the even larger claims occasionally made on his behalf—he may be the humanists' favorite, but he is certainly not Golding's.

To fail to acknowledge in full Simon's role in the story is to be another Polyphemus, seeing only in part what is wholly present. It seems incredible that Simon should be faulted and found wanting because of an alleged inability to communicate.[13] It is true that the other boys think he is talking nonsense, but, as Golding himself says, people at the time of Copernicus thought he, too, was talking nonsense; is the visionary to blame for not being understood? (*Hot Gates*, 38–39). Golding's chief concern—it is he who says so—is with the defects of man, not those of society, because man is for him more important than society. Simon is again the decisive figure; when he goes apart to meditate alone, Golding is affirming the superiority of man to men, upholding what Orwell's totalitarians condemn as the heresy of *ownlife*.

This is an auspicious point on which to end this study. Salvation exists only and inviolably within man himself, the individual human being transcending all social roles, however important they may be. If society is good, so much the better, but even if it is bad, there is no cause for despair. Here, finally, is the most uplifting instance of doubleness, of redemptive equivocation, in *Lord of the Flies*. The text, in the tradition of the dark epiphany, provides one of the most striking and memorable disclosures of the darkness of man's heart; but, simultaneously, in the person of Simon, it supplies the balancing, compensating alternative of a brightness within. It would be presumptuous to demand more. Dame Julian may seem altogether too serene for a troubled century like ours; but, if we cannot be certain of salvation, perhaps it is enough to sustain us if we know that the darkness need not prevail.

Notes and References

Chronology

1. Jack I. Biles, *Talk: Conversations with William Golding* (New York: Harcourt Brace Jovanovich, 1970), 84, 49; hereafter cited in the text.

1. The Missing Master

1. Frank Kermode, *Puzzles and Epiphanies: Essays and Reviews, 1958–1961* (London: Routledge and Kegan Paul, 1962), 213; hereafter cited in the text.

2. Quoted in *William Golding: Novels, 1954–67,* ed. Norman Page (Basingstoke and London: Macmillan, 1985), 23; hereafter cited in the text.

3. Angus Wilson, *Diversity and Depth in Fiction: Selected Critical Writings of Angus Wilson,* ed. Kerry McSweeney (London: Secker and Warburg, 1983), 21–22, 240–41, 243–44; hereafter cited in the text.

4. Anthony Burgess, *The Novel Now* (New York: Norton, 1967), 205.

5. William Golding, *The Hot Gates and Other Occasional Pieces* (London: Faber and Faber, 1965; New York: Harcourt, 1966), 101; hereafter cited in the text.

6. William Golding, *A Moving Target* (London: Faber and Faber, 1982), 163; hereafter cited in the text.

7. Samuel Hynes, *William Golding* (New York and London: Columbia University Press, 1964), 3; hereafter cited in the text.

8. David Magarshack, Introduction to Fyodor Dostoevsky, *The Brothers Karamazov,* trans. David Magarshack (Harmondsworth, Middlesex: Penguin, 1958), xxi–xxii.

9. Frank Kermode, "The Meaning of It All," *Books and Bookmen,* October 1959, 9. See also *A Moving Target,* 183.

10. Dostoevsky, 77.

11. See also D. M. Davis, "A Conversation with William Golding," *New Republic*, 4 May 1963, 28.

12. Quoted in Arnold Johnston, *Of Earth and Darkness: The Novels of William Golding* (Columbia, Mo., and London: University of Missouri Press, 1980), 17; hereafter cited in the text.

13. *Lord of the Flies* (London: Faber and Faber, 1958), 47; hereafter cited in the text.

14. Henry David Rosso, Interview with William Golding, *Ann Arbor News*, 5 December 1985; hereafter cited in the text.

15. James R. Baker, "The Decline of Lord of the Flies," *South Atlantic Quarterly* 69 (1970): 447.

16. Maurice L. McCullen, "*Lord of the Flies*: The Critical Quests" in *William Golding: Some Critical Considerations*, ed. Jack I. Biles and Robert O. Evans (Lexington, Ky.: University Press of Kentucky, 1978), 225.

17. James R. Baker, *William Golding: A Critical Study* (New York: St. Martin's Press, 1965), xvii.

2. The Importance of the Work

1. George Orwell, *The Collected Essays, Journalism and Letters of George Orwell*, ed. Sonia Orwell and Ian Angus (Harmondsworth, Middlesex: Penguin, 1970), 2:170–71.

2. Martin Green, "Distaste for the Contemporary," *Nation* 190 (21 May 1960): 454; hereafter cited in the text.

3. Iris Murdoch, "Against Dryness," in *The Novel Today: Contemporary Writers on Modern Fiction*, ed. Malcolm Bradbury (Glasgow: Fontana-Collins, 1977), 26; hereafter cited in the text.

3. Critical Reception

1. Quoted in Virginia Tiger, *William Golding: The Dark Fields of Discovery* (London: Calder and Boyars, 1974), 38; hereafter cited in the text.

2. Louis Halle, in *William Golding's "Lord of the Flies": A Source Book*; ed. William Nelson (New York: Odyssey, 1963), 6; hereafter cited in the text.

3. G. C. Herndl, "Golding and Salinger: A Clear Choice," *Wiseman Review*, no. 52 (Winter 1964–65): 309–22; John Peter "The Fables of William Golding," *Kenyon Review* 19, no. 4 (Autumn 1957): 582.

4. Matez Muzina, "William Golding: Novels of Extreme Situations," *Studia Romanica et Anglica*, nos. 27–28 (July–December 1969): 43–66; Da-

Notes and References

vid Spitz, "Power and Authority: An Interpretation of Golding's *Lord of the Flies*," *Antioch Review* 30, no. 1 (Spring, 1970): 21–33.

5. Leon Levitt, "Trust the Tale: A Second Reading of *Lord of the Flies*," *English Journal*, April 1969, 521; Maurice L. McCullen, "Lord of the Flies: The Critical Quest," in *William Golding: Some Critical Considerations*, ed. Jack I. Biles and Robert O. Evans (Lexington, Ky.: University Press of Kentucky, 1978), 225.

6. James R. Baker, *William Golding: A Critical Study* (New York: St. Martin's Press, 1965); Bernard F. Dick, *William Golding*, Twayne's English Author Series, no. 57 (New York: Twayne, 1967).

7. Peter Green, "The World of William Golding," *Review of English Literature* 1, no. 2 (April 1960): 62–72. See 63, 68, 71. (1963): 37–57; hereafter cited in the text.

8. Paul Elmen, "Prince of the Devils," *Christianity and Crisis*, 4 February 1963, 7–10.

9. See David Anderson, "Is Golding's Theology Christian?" in *William Golding: Some Critical Considerations*, ed. Jack I. Biles and Robert D. Evans (Lexington, Ky.: University Press of Kentucky 1978), 16.

10. John M. Egan, "Golding's View of Man," *America*, 26 January 1963, 140–41; Francis E. Kearns, "Salinger and Golding: Conflict on the Campus," *America*, 26 January 1963, 136–39; Angus Wilson, *Diversity*, 247.

11. Luke M. Grande, "The Appeal of Golding," *Commonweal*, 25 January 1963, 457–59 Edmund Fuller, "Behind the Vogue: A Rigorous Understanding," *New York Herald Tribune Book Week*, 4 November 1962, 3.

12. R. C. Townsend, "Lord of the Flies: Fool's Gold?" in *Journal of General Education* 16, no.2 (July 1964): 153–60.

13. Leo Tolstoy, *Tolstoy's Letters*, Vol. 1, *1828–1879*, ed. and trans. R. F. Christian (London: Athlone Press, 1978), 211.

14. Bernard S. Oldsey and Stanley Weintraub, *The Art of William Golding* (1965; reprint, Bloomington: Indiana University Press, 1968), 36, hereafter cited in the text.

15. John Peter, "The Fables of William Golding," *Kenyon Review* 19 (Autumn 1957): 578; hereafter cited in the text.

16. Juliet Mitchell, "Concepts and Technique in William Golding," *New Left Review*, May–June 1962, 63–71; John Wain, "The Conflict of Forms in Contemporary English Literature: Part 2," *Critical Quarterly* 4 (Summer 1962): 101–19; James Gindin, "Gimmick and Metaphor in the Novels of William Golding," *Modern Fiction Studies* 6 (Summer 1960): 145–52.

17. Frank Kermode, "The Later Golding," in *Continuities* (London: Routledge and Kegan Paul, 1968), 189.

18. C. B. Cox, "On *Lord of the Flies*," *Critical Quarterly* 2 (1960):

113–14; Hynes, *William Golding*, 4–5, 14–15; Mark Kinkead-Weekes and Ian Gregor, *William Golding: A Critical Study* (London: Faber, 1967), 19, 67–68; according to David Skilton, "His persons and things are primarily persons and things, and do not stand for something else" (reprinted in Page, *William Golding: Novels*, 154).

19. Henri Talon, "Irony in *Lord of the Flies*," *Essay in Criticism* 18, no. 3 (July 1968): 296.

20. Jonathan Swift, *Gulliver's Travels*, ed. Peter Dixon and John Chalker (Harmondsworth, Middlesex: Penguin, 1967), 230–31, hereafter cited in the text.

21. James R. Baker, "An Interview with William Golding," *Twentieth Century Literature* 28 (1982): 131–32, 165.

22. W. B. Yeats, *Mythologies* (London: Macmillan, 1959), 331.

4. Gulliver's Legacy

1. Patrick Reilly, *The Literature of Guilt: From "Gulliver" to Golding* (Basingstoke and London: Macmillan, 1988; Iowa City: University of Iowa Press, 1988), 1–14.

2. Dame Julian of Norwich, *Revelations of Divine Love Recorded by Julian of Norwich*, ed. Grace Warrack (London: Methuen, 1901), 57; hereafter cited in the text.

3. Jean-Paul Sartre, *What Is Literature?* (London: Methuen, 1950), 160–62.

4. George Orwell, *Nineteen Eighty-four* (Harmondsworth, Middlesex: Penguin, 1987), 213.

5. Thomas Mann, *Doctor Faustus*, trans. H. T. Lowe-Porter (Harmondsworth, Middlesex: Penguin, 1971), 458–59.

6. Albert Camus, *The Myth of Sisyphus*, trans. Justin O'Brien (Harmondsworth, Middlesex: Penguin, 1975), 42.

7. Jonathan Swift, *The Correspondence of Jonathan Swift*, ed. Harold Williams (Oxford: Oxford University Press, 1963), 3: 183; hereafter cited in the text as *Correspondence*.

8. Peter Gay, *The Party of Humanity: Essays in the French Enlightenment* (New York: Knopf, 1964), 111–13, 114–16.

9. Jonathan Swift, *The Prose Works of Jonathan Swift*, ed. Herbert Davis (Oxford: Basil Blackwell, 1957), 4:251; hereafter cited in the text as *Prose*.

10. Jonathan Swift, *The Poems of Jonathan Swift*, ed. Harold Williams

Notes and References

(Oxford: Oxford University Press, 1957), 2: 497; hereafter cited in the text as *Poems*.

11. Reinhold Niebuhr, *The Nature and Destiny of Man* (London: Nisbet, 1946), 1:100–101.

12. A. E. Housman, *Collected Poems* (Harmondsworth, Middlesex: Penguin, 1956), 22.

13. William Golding, *Free Fall* (Harmondsworth, Middlesex: Penguin, 1963), 171.

14. Bertrand Russell, *Fact and Fiction* (London: Unwin, 1961), 32.

15. Sigmund Freud, "Thoughts for the Times on War and Death," in *Civilization, Society and Religion* (Harmondsworth, Middlesex: Penguin, 1985), 61–89.

16. D. M. Davis, "A Conversation with William Golding," *New Republic*, 4 May 1963, 28.

17. Quoted in "Lord of the Campus," *Time* 529 (22 June 1962): 64.

18. Albert Camus, *The Fall*, trans. Justin O'Brien (Harmondsworth, Middlesex: Penguin, 1957), 80–81, 82.

19. "It's a Long Way to Oxyrhynchus," *Spectator*, 7 July 1961, 9.

20. "Androids All," *Spectator*, 24 February 1961, 263.

21. Jonathan Swift, *A Tale of a Tub, with Other Early Works, 1696–1707*, ed. Herbert Davis (Oxford: Basil Blackwell, 1965), 102–14.

22. "Who will save the adult and his cruiser?" (Golding's own words, quoted by Epstein) in *Lord of the Flies*, ed. E. L. Epstein (New York: Capricorn Books, 1959), 189.

23. Arthur Miller, Introduction to *Collected Plays* (New York and London: Viking Press, 1957), 44.

24. William Golding, *Pincher Martin* (Harmondsworth, Middlesex; Penguin, 1965), 183.

25. Aldous Huxley, "Wordsworth in the Tropics," *Collected Essays* (New York: Harper and Row, 1960; London: Chatto and Windus, 1960), 1–10; reprinted in *Modern British Literature*, ed. Frank Kermode and John Hollander (London and Toronto: Oxford University Press, 1973), 576–83.

26. James Boswell, *Boswell's Life of Johnson* (London and New York: Dutton, 1967), 1:530.

27. William Shakespeare, *The Winter's Tale*, 2.1.45.

28. James Gindin, *Postwar British Fiction* (Berkeley: University of California Press, 1962); see also James Gindin, "Gimmick and Metaphor in the Novels of William Golding," *Modern Fiction Studies* 6 (Summer 1960): 145–52.

5. Caliban's Freedom

1. Henry James, *Hawthorne* (London: Macmillan; New York: St. Martin's Press, 1967), 55.

2. Mikhail Bakunin, quoted in *The Anarchist Reader*, ed. George Woodcock (Glasgow: Fontana-Collins, 1977), 84.

3. V. S. Pritchett, "Secret Parables," *New Statesman*, 2 August 1958, 146.

4. Kingsley Amis, "William Golding's *Pincher Martin*," *Spectator*, 9 November 1956, 656.

5. Flannery O'Connor, *Mystery and Manners*, ed. Sally and Robert Fitzgerald (New York: Farrar, Strauss and Giroux, 1957), 113–14.

6. Willa Cather, *Not Under Forty* (Lincoln and London: University of Nebraska Press, 1988), 46–47; hereafter cited in the text.

7. W. H. Auden, *W. H. Auden: A Selection*, ed. Richard Hoggart (London: Hutchinson, 1963), 105–6.

8. Saul Bellow, *Henderson the Rain King* (Harmondsworth, Middlesex: Penguin, 1966), 40.

9. Philip Larkin, *The Whitsun Weddings* (London and Boston: Faber and Faber, 1971), 10.

10. Virginia Woolf, *The Common Reader*, 1st ser. (London: Hogarth Press, 1945), 193.

11. John Middleton Murry, *Fyodor Dostoevsky: A Critical Study* (London: Martin Secker, 1923), 39.

12. Fyodor Dostoevsky, *Crime and Punishment*, trans. David Magarshack (Harmondsworth, Middlesex: Penguin, 1958), 482.

13. George Steiner, *Real Presences: Is There Anything in What We Say?* (London and Boston: Faber and Faber, 1989), 12–14.

14. A. C. Swinburne, *Swinburne*, The Penguin Poets (Harmondsworth, Middlesex: Penguin, 1961), 99.

15. Leszek Kolakowski, *Religion: If There Is No God . . . On God, the Devil, Sin and Other Worries of the So-called Philosophy of Religion* (Glasgow: Fontana-Collins, 1982), 201.

16. John Milton, *Paradise Lost*, book 1, ll. 258–59, 263.

17. William Shakespeare, *The Tempest*, 2.1.186.

18. Edmund Burke, *Reflections on the Revolution in France*, ed. Conor Cruise O'Brien (Harmondsworth, Middlesex, Penguin 1969), 91.

19. Denis Diderot, *Rameau's Nephew* and *D'Alembert's Dream*, trans. L. W. Tancock (Harmondsworth, Middlesex: Penguin, 1966), 113.

20. Dante Alighieri, *The Divine Comedy, 1: Hell*, trans. Dorothy L. Sayers (Harmondsworth, Middlesex: Penguin 1954), 101.

Notes and References

21. William Shakespeare, *King Lear*, 5.3.156–57.

22. Christopher Marlowe, *Doctor Faustus*, ed. Roma Gill (London: Ernest Benn, 1978; New York: W. W. Norton, 1978), 19.

23. William Shakespeare, *King Lear*, 4.2.46–49.

24. "I agree that Copernicus' opinion need not be more closely examined. But this: it affects our whole life to know whether the soul is mortal or immortal." Blaise Pascal, *Pensées*, trans. A. J. Krailsheimer (Harmondsworth, Middlesex: Penguin, 1966), 82.

25. Fyodor Dostoyevsky, *The Idiot*, trans. David Magarshack (Harmondsworth, Middlesex: Penguin, 1967), 24.

26. See also *Paradise Lost*, book 2, ll. 5–6.

6. Janus's Island

1. Hannah Arendt, *The Origins of Totalitarianism* (London: Andre Deutsch, 1986), vii.

2. William Shakespeare, *Hamlet*, 2.2.303–5.

3. *Rubaiyat of Omar Khayyam*, trans. Edward Fitzgerald, ed. George F. Maine (Glasgow and London: Collins, 1976), 84.

4. W. E. Channing, quoted in Miguel de Unamuno, *The Tragic Sense of Life* (London and Glasgow: Fontana-Collins, 1962), 90.

5. Sir Thomas Browne, *The Major Works*, ed. C. A. Patrides (Harmondsworth, Middlesex: Penguin, 1977), 103.

6. Alexander Pope, *The Poems of Alexander Pope*, ed. John Butt (London: Methuen, 1968), 516.

7. Herman Melville, *Billy Budd, Sailor and Other Stories* (Harmondsworth, Middlesex: Penguin, 1967), 138.

8. William Shakespeare, *The Tempest*, 5.1.275–76.

9. Sigmund Freud, *Civilization and Its Discontents*, trans. Joan Rivière, ed. James Strachey (London: Hogarth Press, 1975), 23, 24, 59, 65–66, 71.

10. Shakespeare, *The Tempest*, 3.2.136–37.

11. John Webster, *The Duchess of Malfi*, ed. Elizabeth M. Brennan (London: Ernest Benn, 1977; New York: W. W. Norton, 1977), 66.

12. Sophocles, *The Three Theban Plays: Antigone, Oedipus the King, Oedipus at Colonus*, trans. Robert Fagles (Harmondsworth, Middlesex: Penguin, 1984), 85.

13. Harry H. Taylor, "The Case against William Golding's Simon-Piggy," *Contemporary Review*, September 1966, 155–60.

SELECTED BIBLIOGRAPHY

Primary Works

Poems. London: Macmillan, 1934: Reprint. New York: Macmillan, 1935.

Lord of the Flies. London: Faber, 1954: Reprint. New York: Coward-McCann, 1955.

The Inheritors. London: Faber, 1955: Reprint. New York: Harcourt, 1962.

Pincher Martin. London: Faber, 1956. Reprinted as *The Two Deaths of Christopher Martin.* New York: Harcourt, 1957.

Envoy Extraordinary. In *Sometime, Never: Three Tales of Imagination,* by William Golding, John Wyndham, Mervyn Peake. London: Eyre and Spottiswoode, 1956: Reprint. New York: Ballantine Books, 1957.

The Brass Butterfly. London: Faber, 1958: Reprint. In *The Genius of the Later English Theatre,* edited by Sylvan Barnet, Morton Berman, and William Burto. New York: New American Library, 1962.

Free Fall. London: Faber, 1959. Reprint. New York: Harcourt, 1960.

The Spire. London: Faber, 1964. Reprint. New York: Harcourt, 1964.

The Hot Gates and Other Occasional Pieces. London: Faber 1965. Reprint. New York: Harcourt, 1966.

The Pyramid. London: Faber, 1967. Reprint. New York: Harcourt, 1967.

The Scorpion God. London: Faber, 1971. Reprint. New York: Harcourt, 1972.

Darkness Visible. London: Faber, 1979. Reprint. New York: Farrar, Straus and Giroux, 1979.

Rites of Passage. London: Faber, 1980. Reprint. New York: Farrar, Straus and Giroux, 1980.

A Moving Target. London: Faber, 1982. Reprint. New York: Farrar, Straus and Giroux, 1982.

The Paper Men. London: Faber, 1984. Reprint. New York: Farrar, Straus and Giroux, 1984.

An Egyptian Journal. London: Faber, 1985.

Close Quarters. London: Faber, 1987. Reprint. New York: Farrar, Straus and Giroux, 1987.

Fire Down Below. London: Faber, 1989.

Secondary Works

Books

Babb, Howard S. *The Novels of William Golding.* Columbus: Ohio State University Press, 1971. Grounds a discussion of Golding's achievement in an exploration of his narrative and prose style; finds him to be a major novelist despite alleged deficiencies as a creator of character.

Baker, James R. *William Golding: A Critical Study.* New York: St. Martin's Press, 1965. Argues that Golding adapts the techniques of the Greek tragedians, but faults *Lord of the Flies* as a retreat into allegory from the problems of modern life.

Biles, Jack I. *Talk: Conversations with William Golding.* New York: Harcourt, 1970. Provides valuable insights into the novels, with Golding commenting illuminatingly on his own work.

Biles, Jack I., and Robert Evans, eds. *William Golding: Some Critical Considerations.* Lexington, Ky.: University Press of Kentucky, 1978. A very useful collection of essays on different novels and on different aspects of Golding's work, with a valuable bibliography.

Boyd, S. J. *The Novels of William Golding.* Brighton: Harvester Press, 1988. Sensible and illuminating study, with a good chapter on *Lord of the Flies*, relating it to *King Lear* and *Gulliver's Travels.*

Dick, Bernard F. *William Golding.* Twayne's English Author Series, no. 57. New York: Twayne, rev. ed., 1987. A balanced and judicious introduction to the novels; Dick finds in them a "polarity of moral tension"—rational-Apollonian, as opposed to irrational-Dionysian elements.

Elmen, Paul. *William Golding: A Critical Essay.* Contemporary Writers in Christian Perspective. Grand Rapids, Mich.: Eerdmans, 1967. Analyzes Golding against a backdrop of the Fall, political allegory, and Freudian insights. Argues that Golding sees evil within man, but fails to see that evil is also transcendental, too powerful for isolated man to resist.

Gindin, James. *William Golding.* Basingstoke and London: Macmillan, 1988.

A good general survey of Golding's career, with a helpful introductory chapter on background themes and a chapter dealing with *Lord of the Flies* and *The Inheritors*. Sees Golding as "always a strikingly visual writer, evoking physical sensation," and his prose as "a remarkable blend of the abstract and the concrete."

Hodson, Leighton. *William Golding*. Writers and Critics, no. 61. Edinburgh: Oliver and Boyd, 1969. Reprint. New York: Capricorn, 1971. A useful introduction, presenting *Lord of the Flies* as a philosophical or religious work, the central metaphor of which is darkness.

Hynes, Samuel. *William Golding*. Columbia Essays on Modern Writers, no. 2. New York: Columbia University Press, 1964. Presents Golding as a writer who shows not the concerns of the moment but what is basic in the human condition—his greatest gift is to make characters exemplify abstractions without *becoming* abstractions.

Johnston, Arnold. *Of Earth and Darkness: The Novels of William Golding*. Columbia, Mo. and London: University of Missouri Press, 1980. An impressive and important study, which finds *Lord of the Flies* displaying "mythopoeic power" of an impressively high order, and sees the first of Golding's "portraits of the artist" in the depiction of Simon.

Kinkead-Weekes, Mark, and Ian Gregor. *William Golding: A Critical Study*. London: Faber, 1967. Reprint. New York: Harcourt, 1968. An impressive discussion of Golding's achievement, grounded upon an analysis of his narrative and prose style.

Medcalf, Stephen. *William Golding*. Writers and Their Work, no. 243. London: Longman, 1975. Presents Golding as rooted in an English tradition of radical patriotism, employing a prose verging on poetry and contriving to preserve in maturity all the interests of an intelligent English schoolboy.

Moody, Philippa. *A Critical Commentary on William Golding: "Lord of the Flies."* Critical Commentaries for Australian Schools. North Adelaide Australian Letters Publications, 1964. Reprint. London: Macmillan, 1966. Short, sensible introduction, placing *Lord of the Flies* in the context of the contemporary novel.

Nelson, William, ed. *William Golding's "Lord of the Flies": A Source Book*. New York: Odyssey, 1963. An extremely useful collection of early reviews and critical essays on Golding's first and most famous novel.

Oldsey, Bernard S., and Stanley Weintraub. *The Art of William Golding*. New York: Harcourt, 1965. Reprint. Bloomington: Indiana University Press, 1968. Treats Golding's fiction in terms of its "reactive" nature and describes him as a "reactionary," a literary counterpuncher, who is at once both original and derivative.

Page, Norman, ed. *William Golding: Novels, 1954–67*. Basingstoke and London: Macmillan, 1985. A valuable collection of essays on *Lord of the Flies, The Inheritors, Pincher Martin, Free Fall, The Spire,* and *The Pyramid.* Provides both general-survey essays and essays on individual novels by leading Golding critics.

Tiger, Virginia. *William Golding: The Dark Fields of Discovery.* London: Calder and Boyars, 1974. A stimulating book with a good chapter on *Lord of the Flies,* which, Tiger insists, is not allegorically simple but instead ideographically suggestive. The confrontation scenes in the novel reveal a parallel between the boys' disintegrating society and the adult world.

Whitley, John S. *Golding: "Lord of the Flies."* Studies in English Literature, no. 42. London: Edward Arnold, 1970. Places the novel in historical perspective and synthesizes the discussions concerning characterization, fable, and conclusion.

Wilson, Raymond. *Lord of the Flies.* Macmillan Master Guides. Basingstoke and London: Macmillan, 1986. A useful undergraduate introduction, providing a chapter-by-chapter discussion and an analysis of the characters, style, and imagery.

Articles and Parts of Books

Alcantara-Dimalanta, O. "Christian Dimensions in Contemporary Literature." *Unitas* 46 (1973): 213–23. Sets *Lord of the Flies* against a background of contemporary theological thought.

Allen, Walter. *The Modern Novel in Britain and the United States.* Harmondsworth: Penguin, 1965. Credits Golding—in a chapter devoted to him—as the author of powerful books, but notes the weaknesses normal to and perhaps inevitable in allegorical fiction.

Anderson, David. "Is Golding's Theology Christian?" In Biles and Evans, eds., 1–20, *William Golding.* Golding gives us new ways of imaging Christian doctrine, mythological enactments that are also in an important sense the modern equivalents of the archetypal stories in Genesis—what he reformulates is recognizably the mainstream of Christian tradition.

Anderson, Robert S. " 'Lord of the Flies' on Coral Island." *Canadian Review of Sociology and Anthropology* 4, no. 1 (February 1967): 54–69. Examines the relationship between Golding and Ballantyne.

Babb, Howard S. "Four Passages from William Golding's Fiction." *Minnesota Review* 5 (January–April 1965): 50–58. A stylistic analysis of Golding's prose styles taken from four different novels.

Baker, James R. "Why It's No Go: A Study of William Golding's *Lord of the Flies.*" *Arizona Quarterly* 19 (Winter 1963): 293–305. Argues that the

Greeks are more important than Christianity in shaping Golding's conception of psychology and fate, and, in particular, explicates Simon's
death in *Lord of the Flies* by relating it to the orgiastic slaughter in *The
Bacchae.*

———. "The Decline of *Lord of the Flies.*" *South Atlantic Quarterly* 69
(Autumn 1970): 446–60. Argues that Golding had finely dramatized
anxieties common to a postwar world, but that his vogue was now over,
the popularity of his most "relevant fable" in decline.

———. "Golding's Progress." *Novel* 7 (Fall 1973): 62–70. A survey of the
early novels.

———."An Interview with William Golding" *Twentieth Century Literature*
28 (1982): 131–65. Notes that those who regard Golding as an essentially
"poetic" novelist, his novels as dramatic poems, can point as evidence to
his claim to rank Shakespeare as a great forerunner.

Biles, Jack I. "Piggy: Apologia Pro Vita Sua." *Studies in the Literary Imagination* 1 (October 1968): 83–109. A defense of Piggy provoked by Golding's
dismissal of him as the kind of person who ends up in docile, unquestion-
ing service at Los Alamos. Argues that Piggy is the truly multifaceted
character in the book who evades Golding's intentions for him.

———. "Literary Sources and William Golding." *South Atlantic Bulletin* 37
(May 1972): 29–36. A valuable analysis of a writer variously described
as a literary counterpuncher, a "reactionary," and "the supreme abrogator in modern fiction."

Boyle, Ted. E. "Golding's Existential Vision." In Biles and Evans, eds., *William
Golding*, 21–38. Argues that the horror of human existence without
controls or checks is the most consistent theme in Golding; the checks
are arbitrary—yet, when man denies them, his existence is contemptible.

Braybrook, Neville. "Two William Golding Novels: Two Aspects of His
Work." *Queen's Quarterly* 76 (Spring 1969): 92–100. Deals with
mythic and allegorical meanings in *Lord of the Flies* and *Pincher Martin*, finding both novels more complex than simplistic interpretations
generally allow.

Bufkin, E. C. "*Lord of the Flies*: An Analysis." *Georgia Review* 19 (Spring
1965): 40–57. Demonstrates Golding's use of classical irony, Miltonic
imagery, and Jungian archetypes to highlight an opposition between order
and disorder.

Burgess, Anthony. "Golding Unbuttoned." *Listener* 717, 4 November 1964.
Sees Golding as "a baroque bearded mythic visionary, frowning at some
terrible landscape of the mind."

———. "Religion and the Arts: 1—The Manicheans." *Times Literary Supple-*

ment, 3 March 1966, 153–54. Joins Angus Wilson in suggesting that Golding's work is best understood against a background of the omnipotence of evil.

————. *The Novel Now.* New York: Norton, 1967. Some interesting pages on Golding as novelist, remarking (and deploring) the fact that many readers go no further than *Lord of the Flies.*

Cixous-Berger, Helene. "L'allegorie du mal dans l'oeuvre de William Golding." *Critique,* no. 227 (April 1968): 309–20. Discusses *Lord of the Flies* as an allegory of the rise and triumph of evil.

Cohn, Alan M. "The Berengaria Allusion in *Lord of the Flies." Notes and Queries* 211, November 1966, 419–20. Shows that either Simon or Golding has mistakenly attributed to Berengaria, Queen of Richard I, the selfless, heroic act performed by Eleanor of Castile, wife of Edward I. The act itself accords with Simon's saintly character.

Conquest, Robert. "Science Fiction and Literature." *Critical Quarterly* 5 (Winter 1963): 355–67. General essay on science fiction, which declares *Lord of the Flies* and *The Inheritors* to be borderline science-fiction novels.

Coskren, Thomas Marcellus. "Is Golding Calvinistic? A More Optimistic Interpretation of the Symbolism Found in *Lord of the Flies." America* 109, 6 July 1963, 18–20. Defends Golding against Catholic charges of despair-mongering; argues that Golding uses the medium of fable to insist upon individual human responsibility.

Cox, C. B. *"Lord of the Flies." Critical Quarterly* 2 (Summer 1960): 112–17. An important and seminal essay proposing Golding as a religious writer for whom "every detail of human life has a religious significance."

Davis, Douglas M. "A Conversation with Golding." *New Republic,* 4 May 1963, 28–30. Golding acknowledges his admiration for Euripides in particular and for classical Greek literature in general; he tells us that for fifteen years after the war he read mainly this.

Delbaere-Garant, Jeanne. "Rhythm and Expansion in *Lord of the Flies."* In Biles and Evans, eds., *William Golding,* 72–86. Regards the island as "a microcosmic stone thrown in the middle of the ocean with waves of evil radiating around it in larger and larger circles."

Dias-Plaja, Fernando. "Naufragos en dos islas: Un paralelo narrativo: Goytisolo y Golding." *Insula,* October 1965, 6. Examines the shipwreck motif in *Lord of the Flies* and in Juan Goytisolo's *Duelo in Paraiso.*

Dick, Bernard F. *"Lord of the Flies* and *The Bacchae." Classical World,* January 1964, 145–46. Argues that Golding found his inspiration in Euripides, with Simon's slaughter modeled upon the killing of Pentheus.

Drew, Philip. "Second Reading." *Cambridge Review* 78, 27 October 1956,

79. Sees the boys in *Lord of the Flies* as representing various instincts or elements of the personality; each has his own gifts but none is a complete person—from this the tragedy flows.

Egan, John M. "Golding's View of Man." *America* 108, 26 January 1963, 140–41. Part of the Catholic attack on Golding as a purveyor of a pessimistic and life-hating art.

Eller, Vernard. "Depravity or Sin?" *Christian Century* 23, 20 November 1963, 1440. A contribution to the debate over whether Golding's book is reconcilable with Christian teaching.

Elmen, Paul. "Prince of the Devils." *Christianity and Crisis* 23, 4 February 1963, 7–10. Attempts to locate *Lord of the Flies* within a context of contemporary Christian thought.

Ely, Sister M. Amanda. "The Adult Image in Three Novels of Adolescent Life." *English Journal* 56, November 1967, 1127–31. Compares the interaction between children and the worlds of adult authority in *Lord of the Flies*, *The Catcher in the Rye*, and *A Separate Peace*.

Epstein, E. L. "Notes on *Lord of the Flies.*" In *William Golding, Lord of the Flies*. New York: Capricorn Books, 1959. Argues for the relevance of Freudian psychoanalytic theory to *Lord of the Flies*: Golding presents not the traditional devil, but the anarchic, amoral, driving force of the id.

Evans, Robert O. "The Inheritors: Some Inversions." in Biles and Evans, eds., 87–102, *William Golding*. Describes Golding's literary strategy of turning ordinary matters inside out and observing them from a startling point of view—reversing the formula.

Forster, E. M. Introduction to *Lord of the Flies*. New York: Coward, McCann, and Geoghegan, 1962, ix–xii. Prefers Piggy to the other boys, seeing him as symbolic of "the human spirit, aware that the universe has not been created for his convenience."

Freedman, Ralph. "The New Realism: The Fancy of William Golding." *Perspective* 10 (Summer–Autumn 1958): 118–28. An early essay recognizing Golding as a major writer and outlining philosophical and religious approaches that later critics will expand upon.

Furbank, P. N. "Golding's Spire." *Encounter* 22, May 1964, 59–61. Regards *Lord of the Flies* as "still his one perfect novel," because of an alleged inhibition that prevents Golding from handling any but adolescent or preadolescent relationships freely.

Gaskin, J. C. A. "Beelzebub." *Hibbert Journal* 66 (Winter 1967–68): 58–61. Discusses Golding's modern rendition of the devil.

Gindin, James. " 'Gimmick' and Metaphor in the Novels of William Golding." *Modern Fiction Studies* 6 (Summer 1960): 145–52. An important essay in launching the attack upon the allegedly contrived and ultimately "cheating" endings of the novels—e.g., the "rescue" at the close of *Lord of the Flies*. See also James Gindin, *Postwar British Fiction* (Berkeley, Calif.: University of California Press, 1962).

Gordon, Robert C. "Classical Themes in *Lord of the Flies*." *Modern Fiction Studies* 11 (Winter 1965–66): 424–27. Argues that the alleged "gimmick" ending derives from the climax of Euripides' *Orestes*, with Apollo's entry prefiguring that of the naval officer.

Grande, Luke M. "The Appeal of Golding." *Commonweal*, 25 January 1963, 457–59. A Catholic response to attacks by his religious compatriots on *Lord of the Flies*, defending Golding for emphasizing individual moral responsibility over environmental determinism.

Green, Martin. "Distaste for the Contemporary." *Nation* 190 (21 May 1960): 451–54. Attacks Golding as a kind of intellectual Luddite, enviously resentful of scientific progress and prestige in the modern world.

Green, Peter. "The World of William Golding." *Review of English Literature* 1 no. 2 (April 1960): 62–72. An important and influential survey-review, proposing Golding as a religious novelist, the framework of whose novels is conceived in terms of traditional Christian symbolism.

Gregor, Ian, and Mark Kinkead-Weekes. "The Strange Case of Mr. Golding and His Critics." *Twentieth Century 167*, February 1960, 115–25. Argues that Golding's books are about the myth of paradise lost. In the earlier novels (up to *Free Fall*) we find the deliberate isolation of strongly defined subjects from the mesh of complicating circumstance that surround them in "real life." The novel's mythic structure enables Golding continually to direct our attention to Man, rather than "a man" or the relationships of men.

Gulbin, Suzanne. "Parallels and Contrasts in *Lord of the Flies* and *Animal Farm*." *English Journal 55*, January 1966, 86. An examination of the relationship between the two allegories.

Halle, Louis J. "Small Savages." *Saturday Review* 38, no. 42 (15 October, 1955): 16. Faults the ending as a playwright's contrivance for bringing down the curtain and finds the novelist's vision conflicting with that of the textbook anthropologist.

Harvey, W. J. "The Reviewing of Contemporary Fiction." *Essays in Criticism* 8 (April 1958): 182–87. Compares *Pincher Martin* with *Lord of the Flies* and finds the latter to be superior, citing the beautifully pointed irony of the last paragraph as evidence.

Herndl, George C. "Golding and Salinger: A Clear Choice." *Wiseman Review*, no. 502 (Winter 1964–65): 309–22. Places *Lord of the Flies* within the classical and Christian traditions to present it as "an implicit tribute to the humanizing power of social institutions" and a refutation of Rousseauist individualism.

141

Hewitt, Douglas. Review of *Lord of the Flies*. *Manchester Guardian*, 28 September 1954. Praises the book but faults it for a tendency to be too explicit, too schematic, almost diagrammatic.

Hollahan, Eugene. "Running in Circles: A Major Motif in *Lord of the Flies*." *Studies in the Novel* 2 (Spring 1970): 22–30. Argues that Golding's novel is arranged around the concept of two important kinds of circle—the sociopolitical circle of rational discussion and the regressive circle of atavistic tribalism.

Hough, Graham. Review of *Free Fall*. *Listener* 66, 5 November 1959. Praises *Lord of the Flies* for showing Golding at his best, as a writer of fable, of near-allegory.

Hynes, Samuel. "Novels of a Religious Man." *Commonweal* 17, 18 March 1960, 673–75. Presents Golding as a major religious writer in an irreligious age, ingenious in adapting allegory (a traditional form for religious utterance) to contemporary requirements.

————. "The Cost of a Vision." *Times Literary Supplement*, 16 April 1964. Presents Golding as a writer who has designs on us, a moralist in an unmoralistic age, dealing with what is constant in man's nature.

Irwin, Joseph J. "The Serpent Coiled Within." *Motive*, May 1963, 1–5. A survey-criticism from the Protestant viewpoint; argues that Golding's abiding thesis is that man's difficulties stem not from his intellect, but from his nature.

Jennings, Elizabeth. "Golding." *Listener* 71, 9 April 1964. Regards Golding's fiction as dominated by one theme: the borderline between reality and madness.

Josipovici, Gabriel. "William Golding." In *The World and the Book: A Study of Modern Fiction*. Stanford, Calif.: Stanford University Press; London: Macmillan, 1971. Penetrating and illuminating chapter stressing the sense of exploration in Golding: "his strength lies in the violent force of his imagination"—despite his own description of himself as an ideas man.

Karl, Frederick R. "The Novel as Moral Allegory: The Fiction of William Golding," in *A Reader's Guide to the Contemporary English Novel*. New York: Noonday Press, 1962; London, Thames and Hudson, 1963. Rev. ed. New York: Farrar, 1972; Toronto: Doubleday Canada, 1972. Regards Golding's novels as religious allegories in which the conceptual machinery undermines the "felt life" of the tale; the idea is invariably superior to the performance.

Kearns, Francis E. "Salinger and Golding: Conflict on the Campus." *America*, 26 January 1963, 136–39. Laments the displacement of *The Catcher in the Rye*, representing humane liberalism, by *Lord of the Flies*, with its alleged vision of inevitably triumphant depravity.

Kearns, Francis E., and Luke M. Grande. "An Exchange of Views." *Common-*

weal, 22 February 1963, 569–71. Collision between two opposing Catholic views of *Lord of the Flies*: Calvinist pessimism versus Christian humanism.

Kermode, Frank. "Coral Islands." *Spectator*, 22 August 1958, 257. Relates *Lord of the Flies* to Ballantyne's *The Coral Island*, showing how each is the product of radically opposed historical epochs.

———. "The Meaning of It All." *Books and Bookmen*, October 1959, 9–10. Extremely valuable discussion with Golding, supplying helpful hints to an understanding of *Lord of the Flies*.

———. "William Golding." In *Puzzles and Epiphanies: Essays and Reviews 1958–1961*. London: Routledge & Kegan Paul, 1962. Shows Golding reacting against *The Coral Island* argues that the latter could be used as a document in the history of ideas.

———. "The Case for William Golding." *New York Review of Books*, 30 April 1964, 3–4. Reads Golding against a background of Frazer and Freud: *The Golden Bough*, *Totem and Taboo*, *Moses and Monotheism*. Argues that Golding's work is predicated on the theory that individual recapitulates in capsule time the development of the species.

———"The Later Golding." In *Continuities*. London: Routledge & Kegan Paul, 1968. Finds the explanation of *Lord of the Flies*'s vast readership in an ironic handling of the earthly paradise myth.

Lederer, Richard H. "Student Reactions of *Lord of the Flies*." *English Journal* 53, November 1964, 575–79. Plays down the novel's popular appeal and finds its influence to be overrated.

Lederer, Richard H., and Paul Hamilton Beattie. "*African Genesis* and *Lord of the Flies*: Two Studies of the Beastie Within." *English Journal* 58, December 1969, 1316. Shows how the philosophical naturalist and the novelist handle the same questions about human nature and the environment.

Levine, Paul. "Individualism and the Traditional Talent." *Hudson Review* 17 (Autumn 1964): 470–77. Identifies Golding's willingness to attack unhackneyed material as his greatest virtue, while his greatest weakness is an indulgent taste for ponderous allegory.

Levitt, Leon. "Trust the Tale: A Second Reading of *Lord of the Flies*." *English Journal* 58, April 1969, 521. Rejects Golding's view of the book as tracing the defects of society back to the defects of human nature, and finds instead that the book reveals the evil in Western culture.

Lewis, C. S., Brian Aldiss, and Kingsley Amis. "Unreal Estates." *Encounter* 24, March 1965, 61–65. A tripartite discussion of science fiction, with Amis and Aldiss speaking for *Lord of the Flies* as possessing "a science fiction atmosphere," while Lewis denies any relation to science fiction.

Lodge, David. "The Novelist at the Crossroads." *Critical Quarterly* 11 (Summer 1969): 105–32. Rebukes Walter Allen's assumption a propos of *Lord of the Flies* that allegory is necessarily a literary vice and that *Lord of the Flies* is only a rather unpleasant and too easily affecting story.

McCullen, Maurice L. "*Lord of the Flies*: The Critical Quest." In Biles and Evans, eds., 203–36 *William Golding*. A very full and useful survey of critics' views from the book's publication until the late 1970s.

MacLure, Millar. "Allegories of Innocence." *Dalhousie Review* 40 (Summer 1960): 145–56. Propounds the thesis that "the art of this century is haunted by the ghost of innocence," and finds in modern allegory a frustrated longing for exculpation.

MacShane, Frank. "The Novels of William Golding." *Dalhousie Review* 42 (Summer 1962): 171–83. Defends *Lord of the Flies* against charges of exaggeration; presents it as Golding's most accessible novel, horribly realistic, an indictment of society as it brutally is.

Marcus, Steven. "The Novel Again." *Partisan Review* 29 (Spring 1962): 171–95. Hails Golding as the most interestingly imaginative novelist in two decades. His novels are rigorously organized and heavily controlled, using with exact naturalness the findings and doctrines of modern anthropology and psychoanalysis—whatever freedom or spontaneity may be discovered in them resembles the freedom we find in a dramatic poem.

Matuz, Roger, ed. "Golding." In *Contemporary Literary Criticism*, vol. 58. Detroit: Gale Research, 1990. A very useful collection of excerpts from key essays on *Lord of the Flies* up to 1988.

Michel-Michot, Paulette. "The Myth of Innocence." *Revue des langues vivantes* 28, no. 4 (1962): 510–20. Argues that Golding explodes the myth of innocence and takes us back to the problem of evil ignored by Ballantyne and oversimplified by Defoe.

Mitchell, Charles. "*The Lord of the Flies* and the Escape from Freedom." *Arizona Quarterly* 22 (Spring 1966): 27–40. Reads *Lord of the Flies* as confirmation of Erich Fromm's thesis about the flight from freedom in modern history.

Mitchell, Juliet. "Concepts and Techniques in William Golding." *New Left Review*, May–June 1962, 63–71. Attacks Golding's art, in *Lord of the Flies* and elsewhere, as a conjuring trick—a spurious complexity is the result of confusing children with adults.

Muzina, Matej. "William Golding: Novels of Extreme Situations." *Studia Romanica et Anglica*, nos. 27–28 (July–December 1969): 43–66. Argues that Golding is an existentialist who places man in contingent situations in order to test religious and scientific orthodoxies.

Nichols, James W. "Nathanael West, Sinclair Lewis, Alexander Pope and

Selected Bibliography

Satiric Contrasts." *Satire Newsletter* 5 (Spring 1968): 119–22. Treats Golding as a satirist with an optimistic view of the human situation.

Niemeyer, Carl. *"The Coral Island* Revisited." *College English* 22, January 1961, 241–45. Analyzes *Lord of the Flies* as a twentieth-century response to R. M. Ballantyne's boys' adventure story.

Nossen, Evon. "The Beast-Man Theme in the Work of William Golding." *Ball State University Forum* 9 (1968): 60–69. Traces the beast-man theme through Golding's novels to show that his view of man is one of cautious optimism.

Oakland, John. "Satiric Technique in *Lord of the Flies.*" *Moderna Sprak* 64 (1970): 14–18. Argues that Golding's targets are the liberal humanist tradition of rationalist orthodoxy, man's presumption of possible perfection, and his belief in natural goodness and self-sufficiency.

O'Hara, J. D. "Mute Choirboys and Angelic Pigs: The Fable in *Lord of the Flies.*" *Texas Studies in Literature and Language* 7 (Winter 1966): 411–20. Finds the novel irrelevant because "man cannot be cut off completely from his past" and also because man's essential illness is, in fact, attributable in the text merely to the weakness and ignorance of children.

Oldsey, Bernard S., and Stanley Weintraub. *"Lord of the Flies*: Beelzebub Revisted." *College English* 25, November 1963, 90–99. Argues that the main ancestor of *Lord of the Flies* is *Gulliver's Travels* and that Golding's art, like Swift's, straddles the realms of fiction and allegory.

Painter, George D. Review of *Lord of the Flies. Listener* 61, 21 October 1954. Hails *Lord of the Flies* as "a powerful first novel" written "with style and authority."

Pendry, E. D. "William Golding and 'Mankind's Essential Illness.' " *Moderna Sprak* 55 (1961): 1–7. A review-survey of the early novels.

Peter, John. "The Fables of William Golding." *Kenyon Review* 19 (Autumn 1957): 577–92. Important and influential in attempting to define critical terms for an understanding of Golding's work; despite what he sees as overexplicitness in Golding's work, he praises him for having done more for the modern British novel than any other living novelist.

Pritchett, V. S. "Secret Parables." *New Statesman* 56, 2 August 1958, 146–47. Regards *Lord of the Flies* as the most accomplished of Golding's novels: "the pressure of feeling drives allegory out of the foreground of his stories."

Quigley, Isabel. Review of *Lord of the Flies. Spectator*, 30 September 1955. Hails Golding as "the most original and imaginatively exciting novelist we have today," with *Lord of the Flies* as an unrepeatable achievement.

Reilly, Patrick. "Beelzebub's Boys: *Lord of the Flies.*" In *The Literature of Guilt: From "Gulliver" to Golding*, 138–61. London: Macmillan; Iowa City: University of Iowa Press, 1988. Places *Lord of the Flies* in the context of "the dark epiphany," a moment of appalled self-discovery in

145

modern fiction that has its great paradigm in the last voyage of *Gulliver's Travels*.

Rosenberg, Bruce A. "Lord of the Fire-flies." *Centennial Review* 11 (Winter 1967): 128–39. Studies the fire imagery in *Lord of the Flies*, concluding that fire, not the pig's head, is the central symbol.

Rosenfield, Claire. "Men of a Smaller Growth: A Psychological Analysis of William Golding's *Lord of the Flies*." *Literature and Psychology* 11 (Autumn 1961): 93–101. A controversial essay arguing that Golding "consciously dramatizes Freudian theory"—despite Golding's assertion that he had never read Freud.

Rosso, Henry David. Interview with William Golding. *Ann Arbor News*, 5 December 1985. Golding makes the interesting remark that *Lord of the Flies* was written at "a time of great world grief."

Skilton, David. *Studies in the Literary Imagination*, 2 October 1969. Reprinted in *William Golding: Novels 1954–67*, ed. Norman Page, 151–65. Basingstoke and London: Macmillan, 1985. Cautions about the danger of overinterpretation when reading Golding: "his persons and things are primarily persons and things, and do not stand for something else."

Spitz, David. "Power and Authority: An Interpretation of Golding's *Lord of the Flies*." *Antioch Review* 30 (Spring 1970): 21–33. Treats the novel as a work of political theory whose characters (seer, Socratic man, democratic man, authoritarian man) are symbols of diverse responses to the questions of power, legitimacy, and authority.

Stern, James. "English Schoolboys in the Jungle." *New York Times Book Review*, 23 October 1955, 38. Sees *Lord of the Flies* as an allegory showing that civilization is merely skin-deep, with Piggy "the hero of a triumphant literary effort."

Sternlicht, Sanford. "A Source for Golding's *Lord of the Flies*: Peter Pan?" *English Record* 14, no. 2 (December 1963): 41–42. Suggests a possible parallel between the rape of the sow and that of Wendy.

———. "Songs of Innocence and Songs of Experience in *Lord of the Flies* and *The Inheritors*." *Midwest Quarterly* 9 (July 1968): 383–90. Argues that the boys in *Lord of the Flies* are not innocents, but "the new people"— innocence died with Lok in *The Inheritors*.

Sullivan, Walter. "William Golding: The Fables and the Art." *Sewanee Review* 71 (Autumn 1963): 660–64. Dismisses Golding as a fabulist, though a very good one; nevertheless, not even Golding's considerable talent can transcend the limitations of the form. Argues that the fictions are constructed to illustrate preexisting truths.

Talon, Henri A. "Irony in *Lord of the Flies*." *Essays in Criticism* 18 (July 1968): 296–309. Finds in it the irony of a moralist who exposes aberrant conduct and multiform evil but who opens no vista to a world to which men could aspire. The irony of the ending is that the rescue is only a brief respite.

Taylor, Harry H. "The Case against William Golding's Simon-Piggy." *Contemporary Review* 209, no. 1208 (September 1966): 155–60. Assumes that the "Simon-Piggy" figure should be viewed as a "dual hero"; Piggy is the real central figure because Simon's inability to communicate proves his incompleteness.

Thomson, George H. "William Golding: Between God-Darkness and God-Light." *Cresset* 32, vii (June 1969): 8–12. Presents the polarities of grace and pride to show Golding as a writer within the orthodox Christian tradition.

Townsend, R. C. "*Lord of the Flies*: Fool's Gold?" *Journal of General Education* 16 (July 1964): 153–60. One of Golding's most hostile critics, Townsend attacks *Lord of the Flies* as a bad book that manipulates its characters and exploits its young readers in the interests of a boutique despair.

Trilling, Lionel. "*Lord of the Flies*." *Mid-Century*, October 1962, 10–12. Describes the novel as "one of the most striking literary phenomena of recent years," a book that "seems to have captivated the imagination of a whole generation."

Tristram, Philippa. "Golding and the Language of Caliban." In Biles and Evans, eds., 39–55, *William Golding*. Argues that Golding's imagination is drawn to the simplicities of primal myths, and it is through their rediscovery that he seeks to arrive at the truths of his contemporary world.

Veidemanis, Gladys. "*Lord of the Flies* in the Classroom—No Passing Fad." *English Journal* 53, November 1964, 569–74. Challenges the view of those (see Baker) who declare that the appeal of the book is waning, and insists that *Lord of the Flies* deserves a permanent place in the curriculum.

Wain, John. "The Conflict of Forms in Contemporary English Literature: Part 2." *Critical Quarterly* 4 (Summer 1962): 101–19. Argues that Golding is, in a sense, not a novelist at all, but a writer on themes ultimately religious, whose work, when it is successful, has the authority of myth.

Walters, Margaret. "Two Fabulists: Golding and Camus." *Melbourne Critical Review* 4 (1961): 18–29. An important and influential attempt to define the critical terms in which Golding's work is best understood; Walters rejects allegory in favor of fable.

Warner, Oliver. "Mr. Golding and Marryat's *Little Savage*." *Review of English Literature* 5 (January 1964): 51–55. Traces similarities between *Lord of the Flies* and the romance writer Frederick Marryat.

Wasserstrom, William. "Reason and Reverence in Art and Science." *Literature and Psychology* 12 (Winter 1962): 2–5. Uses Claire Rosenfield's Freudian methodology to attack her reading of *Lord of the Flies*.

Watson, Kenneth. "A Reading of *Lord of the Flies*." *English* 15, no. 85 (Spring 1964): 2–7. Pays tribute to the impact of the text on even nonliterary students, but thinks that it has been too often and too easily assumed to be a religious work.

Webster, Owen. "Living with Chaos." *Books and Art*, March 1958, 15–16. An interview with Golding in which he discusses his work.

White, Robert J. "Butterfly and Beast in *Lord of the Flies*." *Modern Fiction Studies* 10 (Summer 1964): 163–70. Argues that *Lord of the Flies* is based on Greek sources, especially *The Republic* and *The Bacchae*; Simon is a scapegoat like Pentheus in Euripides.

Wilson, Angus. "Evil in the English Novel." *Kenyon Review* 29 (March 1967): 167–94. Reprinted in *Diversity and Depth in Fiction: Selected Critical Writings of Angus Wilson*, ed. Kerry McSweeney. London: Secker and Warburg, 1983. Praises Golding for having solved in *Lord of the Flies* the problem of expressing transcendent good and evil more satisfactorily than any other living English novelist.

Young, Wayland. "Letter from London." *Kenyon Review* 19 (Summer 1957): 478–82. Praises *Lord of the Flies* as a timeless story of fear, the tidings, and the blood sacrifice in which the specific Christian elements are always subordinate to a generalized sense of natural religion.

INDEX

Index

LORD OF THE FLIES

Index

Wells, Herbert George, 8, 25, 34,
36, 38, 111
West, Nathanael, 70
Wilson, Angus, 3, 19, 20, 60, 107
Wilson, Harold, 8

Winter's Tale, The, 105, 121
Woolf, Virginia, 64
Wordsworth, William, 46, 100, 104

Yeats, William Butler, 21, 86

THE AUTHOR

Patrick Reilly was born in Glasgow and was educated at the University of Glasgow and Pembroke College, Oxford, where he earned his B. Litt. He is currently a Reader in the English Department at the University of Glasgow. His publications include *Jonathan Swift: The Brave Desponder*, *George Orwell: The Age's Adversary*, and *The Literature of Guilt: From "Gulliver" to Golding*. He is also the author of two other volumes in Twayne's Masterwork Studies Series—*Nineteen Eighty-four: Past, Present, and Future* and *Tom Jones: Adventure and Providence*. A contributor to several books, including six volumes of anthologized literary criticism, Reilly has also published articles on such subjects as Orwell, Joyce, Scottish literature, and education and religion.